Berlitz®

Polish

phrase book & dictionary

KT-479-795

PTTK

BACÓWKA PTTK 15 min.
POD MAŁĄ RAWKĄ

USTRZYKI
DOLNE

POŁONINA
CARYŃSKA
PRZEŁĘCZ
WYZNIAŃSKA

1h

5 min

PTTK

DOLNE

Berlitz Publishing
New York   London   Singapore

Contacting the Editors
Every effort has been made to provide accurate information in this publication, but changes are inevitable. The publisher cannot be responsible for any resulting loss, inconvenience or injury. We would appreciate it if readers would call our attention to any errors or outdated information. We also welcome your suggestions; if you come across a relevant expression not in our phrase book, please contact us at: **comments@berlitzpublishing.com**

All Rights Reserved
© 2007 Berlitz Publishing/APA Publications (UK) Ltd.
Berlitz Trademark Reg. U.S. Patent Office and other countries. Marca Registrada. Used under license from Berlitz Investment Corporation.

Eleventh Printing: March 2012
Printed in China

Publishing Director: Mina Patria
Commissioning Editor: Kate Drynan
Editorial Assistant: Sophie Cooper
Translation: updated by Wordbank
Cover Design: Beverley Speight
Interior Design: Beverley Speight
Production Manager: Raj Trivedi
Picture Researcher: Lucy Johnston
Cover Photo: All photos Corrie Wingate/APA except 'currency' photo iStockphoto; Main 'signpost' photo Gregory Wrona/APA.

Interior Photos: Kevin Cummins/APA 41, 48; iStockphoto 141,144,151, 152, 156, 165; Britta Jaschinski/APA 12, 37, 44; Lucy Johnston/APA 178; Jon Santa Cruz/APA 124,148; Corrie Wingate/APA 19, 24, 30, 65, 70, 81, 86, 100, 103, 110, 115, 117, 122, 130, 162; Gregory Wrona/APA 1, 15, 54, 56, 76, 96, 107, 129, 132,137, 138, 142, 146.

Contents

Food & Drink

People

Leisure Time

Special Requirements

In an Emergency

Dictionary

Pronunciation

This section is designed to familiarize you with the sounds of Polish using our simplified phonetic transcription. You'll find the pronunciation of the Polish letters and sounds explained below, together with their imitated equivalents. To use this system, found throughout the phrase book, simply read the pronunciation as if it were English, noting any special rules below.

Underlined letters indicate that the syllable should be stressed. In Polish, stress falls on the penultimate syllable: *autobus*, *szkoła*. In some words of foreign origin (mostly Latin and Greek), stress is assigned to the third syllable from the end of the word: *uniwersytet*.

Consonants/Consonant Clusters

Letter	Approximate Pronunciation	Symbol	Example	Pronunciation
c	like ts in fits	**ts**	**cały**	*tsah-wyh*
ć, ci	a soft, very short version of chee in cheese	**ch'**	**cień**	*ch'yen'**
cz	like ch in church but harder	**ch**	**czapka**	*chahp-kah*
dz	like ds in beds	**dz**	**dzwonek**	*dzvoh-nehk*
drz, dż	like j in jam	**dj**	**drzwi**	*djvee*
dź, dzi	like ge in genius	**dj'**	**dzień**	*dj'yen'*
h, ch	hard, like the ch in Scottish loch	**h**	**chleb**	*hlehp*
j	like y in yes	**y**	**jutro**	*yoo-troh*
ł	like w in win	**w**	**łóżko**	*woozh-koh*
ń, ni	like ni in onion	**n'**	**nie**	*n'yeh*

r	rolled, distinct at the end of words	r	**rower**	_roh-vehr_
sz	like sh in shot but harder	**sh**	**szkoła**	_shkoh-wah_
ś, si	soft, very short version of shee in sheep	**sh'**	**śmieci**	_sh'myeh-ch'ee_
w	like v in very	**v**	**woda**	_voh-dah_
ź, zi	like s in pleasure but softer	**zh'**	**źródło**	_zh'rood-woh_
ż, rz	like s in pleasure but harder	**zh**	**żaba**	_zhah-bah_

Letters b, d, f, k, l, m, n, p, s, t, z are pronounced approximately as in English.
* The apostrophe (') in phonetics indicates a softening of the sound.

Polish is a language with a long history. Like most other European languages, it has its origin in Sanskrit and is part of the Indo-European group. It is one of 14 Slavic languages.
Polish is a phonetic language - there is a good correlation of sound to spelling - and its pronunciation is much more systematic than that of English.

se this Book

Sometimes you see two alternatives in italics, separated by a slash. Choose the one that's right for your situation.

rzyjechałem *m* **/Przyjechałam** *f* **tutaj na vakacje/służbowo.** *pshyh-yeh-hah-wehm/ shyh-yeh-hah-wahm tuh-tahy nah vah-kahts-yeh/ wuhzh-boh-voh*

adę do... *yah-deh doh...*

atrzymałem *m* **/Zatrzymałam** *f* **się w lotelu...** *zah-tshyh-mah-wehm/ rah-tshyh-mah-wahm sh'yeh fhoh-teh-luh...*

Words you may see are shown in YOU MAY SEE boxes.

life boats
life jackets
deck

Any of the words or phrases listed can be plugged into the sentence below.

) której jest...do Krakowa? *oh ktuh-rehy yehst...doh krah-koh-vah*

pierwszy) autobus *(pyehr-shyh) ahw-toh-buhs*

następny) samolot *(nahs-tehm-pnyh) sah-moh-loht*

ostatni) pociąg *(ohs-taht-n'ee) poh-ch'yonk*

Vowels

Letter
a
e
i
o
u, ó
y
ą
ę

ą
1.
fi
o
2.
be
3.
be

ę
1.
a c
2.
b a
3. e
in a

How to u

ESSENTIAL
I'm here on vacation
[holiday]/business.

I'm going to...
I'm staying at the...
Hotel.

YOU MAY SEE...
ŁODZIE RATUNKOWE
KAPOKI
POKŁAD

Tickets

When's...to Cracow?

the (first) bus
the (next) flight
the (last) train

Polish phrases appear in purple.

Read the simplified pronunciation as if it were English. For more on pronunciation, see page 7.

At the Bank

I'd like to change money.	**Chciałbym** m /**Chciałabym** f **wymienić pieniądze.** hh'yahw•byhm/hch'yah•wah•byhm vyh•myeh•n'eech' pyeh•n'yohn•dzeh
What's the exchange rate?	**Jaki jest kurs wymiany?** yah•kee yehst kurs vyh•myah•yh
How much is the fee? For Numbers, see page 171.	**Jaka jest prowizja?** yah•kah yest proh•veez•yah

Related phrases can be found by going to the page number indicated.

When different gender forms apply, the masculine form is followed by m; feminine by f

When addressing a man in a formal situation, use **pan** (sir); when addressing a woman, use **pani** (ma'am or madam). Throughout this phrase book **pan** is used for the sake of simplicity. When speaking to a woman, be sure to substitute **pani** for **pan**.

Information boxes contain relevant country, culture and language tips.

Expressions you may hear are shown in You May Hear boxes.

YOU MAY HEAR...
Bilet/Paszport, proszę.
bee•leht/pahsh•pohrt proh•sheh

Your ticket/passport, please.

Color-coded side bars identify each section of the book.

Survival

Survival

Polish phrases appear in purple.

Read the simplified pronunciation as if it were English. For more on pronunciation, see page 7.

At the Bank

I'd like to change money.

Chciałbym m /**Chciałabym** f **wymienić pieniądze.** hch'yahw•byhm/hch'yah•wah•byhm vyh•myeh•neech' pyeh•n'yohn•dzeh

What's the exchange rate?

Jaki jest kurs wymiany? yah•kee yehst kurs vyh•myah•yh

How much is the fee?

Jaka jest prowizja? yah•kah yest proh•veez•yah

For Numbers, see page 171.

Related phrases can be found by going to the page number indicated.

When different gender forms apply, the masculine form is followed by m; feminine by f

When addressing a man in a formal situation, use **pan** (sir); when addressing a woman, use **pani** (ma'am or madam). Throughout this phrase book **pan** is used for the sake of simplicity. When speaking to a woman, be sure to substitute **pani** for **pan**.

Information boxes contain relevant country, culture and language tips.

Expressions you may hear are shown in You May Hear boxes.

YOU MAY HEAR...

Bilet/Paszport, proszę.
bee•leht/pahsh•pohrt proh•sheh

Your ticket/passport, please.

Color-coded side bars identify each section of the book.

Vowels

Letter	Approximate Pronunciation	Symbol	Example	Pronunciation
a	like a in father	**ah**	**dach**	*dahh*
e	like e in ten	**eh**	**bez**	*behs*
i	like ee in keen	**ee**	**kino**	*kee-noh*
o	like o in so	**oh**	**okno**	*ohk-noh*
u, ó	like u in put	**oo**	**sufit**	*soo-feet*
y	like i in fit	**yh**	**buty**	*boo-tyh*
ą	1. nasal, like an in fiancé, at the end of a word	**1. ohm**	**1. są**	*1. sohm*
	2. pronounced ohn before a consonant	**2. ohn**	**2. kąt**	*2. kohnt*
	3. pronounced ohm before b and p	**3. ohm**	**3. ząb**	*3. zohmb*
ę	1. ehn before a consonant	**1. ehn**	**1. ręka**	*1. rehn-kah*
	2. ehm before b and p	**2. ehm**	**2. kępa**	*2. kehm-pah*
	3. eh when final in a word	**3. eh**	**3. tę**	*3. teh*

How to use this Book

> Sometimes you see two alternatives in italics, separated by a slash. Choose the one that's right for your situation.

ESSENTIAL

I'm here on vacation [holiday]/business.

Przyjechałem m **/Przyjechałam** f **tutaj na wakacje/służbowo.** *pshyh-yeh-hah-wehm/ pshyh-yeh-hah-wahm tuh-tahy nah vah-kahts-yeh/ swuhzh-boh-voh*

I'm going to...

Jadę do... *yah-deh doh...*

I'm staying at the... Hotel.

Zatrzymałem m **/Zatrzymałam** f **się w Hotelu...** *zah-tshyh-mah-wehm/ zah-tshyh-mah-wahm sh'yeh fhoh-teh-luh...*

> Words you may see are shown in YOU MAY SEE boxes.

YOU MAY SEE...

ŁODZIE RATUNKOWE	life boats
KAPOKI	life jackets
POKŁAD	deck

> Any of the words or phrases listed can be plugged into the sentence below.

Tickets

When's...to Cracow?

O której jest...do Krakowa? *oh ktuh-rehy yehst...doh krah-koh-vah*

the (first) bus

(pierwszy) autobus *(pyehr-shyh) ahw-toh-buhs*

the (next) flight

(następny) samolot *(nahs-tehm-pnyh) sah-moh-loht*

the (last) train

(ostatni) pociąg *(ohs-taht-n'ee) poh-ch'yonk*

Arrival & Departure

ESSENTIAL

I'm here on vacation/ business.	**Przyjechałem** *m* **/Przyjechałam** *f* **tutaj na wakacje/ łużbowo.** *pshyh•yeh•hah•wehm/pshyh•yeh•hah•wahm too•tahy nah vah•kahts•yeh/swoozh•boh•voh*
I'm going to…	**Jadę do…** *yah•deh doh…*
I'm staying at the… Hotel.	**Zatrzymałem** *m* **/Zatrzymałam** *f* **się w Hotelu…** *zah•tshyh•mah•wehm/zah•tshyh•mah•wahm sh'yeh fhoh•teh•loo…*

YOU MAY HEAR...

Bilet/Paszport, proszę. *bee•leht/pahsh•pohrt proh•sheh*	Your ticket/passport, please.
Jaki jest cel pana wizyty? *yah•kee yehst tsehl pah•nah vee•zyh•tyh*	What's the purpose of your visit?
Gdzie pan się zatrzymał? *gdj'yeh pahn sh'yeh zah•tshyh•mahw*	Where are you staying?
Jak długo pan tu będzie? *yahk dwoo•goh pahn too behn•dj'ye*	How long are you staying?
Z kim pan tutaj jest? *skeem pahn too•tahy yehst*	Who are you here with?

When addressing a man in a formal situation, use **pan** (sir); when addressing a woman, use **pani** (ma'am or madam). Throughout this phrase book **pan** is used for the sake of simplicity. When speaking to a woman, be sure to substitute **pani** for **pan**.

Border Control

I'm just passing through.	**Jestem tu tylko przejazdem.** _yeh·stehm too tyhl·koh psheh·yahz·dehm_
I would like to declare...	**Chciałbym _m_ /Chciałabym _f_ zadeklarować...** _hch'yahw·byhm/hch'yah·wah·byhm zah·dehk·lah·roh·vahch'..._
I have nothing to declare.	**Nie mam nic do oclenia.** _n'yeh mahm n'eets doh ohts·leh·n'yah_

YOU MAY HEAR...

Czy ma pan coś do oclenia? _chyh mah pahn tsohsh' doh ohts·leh·n'yah_ — Anything to declare?

Musi pan zapłacić za to cło. _moo·sh'ee pahn zah·pwa·ch'eech' zah toh tswoh_ — You must pay duty on this.

Proszę otworzyć torbę/walizkę. _proh·sheh oht·foh·zhyhch' tohr·beh/vah·lees·keh_ — Please open your bag/suitcase.

YOU MAY SEE...

ODPRAWA CELNA	customs
TOWARY BEZCŁOWE	duty-free goods
TOWARY DO OCLENIA	goods to declare
NIC DO OCLENIA	nothing to declare
KONTROLA PASZPORTOWA	passport control
POLICJA	police
DLA PERSONELU	staff only

Money

ESSENTIAL

Where's…?	**Gdzie jest…?** *gdj'yeh yehst…*
the ATM	**bankomat** *bahn•koh•maht*
the bank	**bank** *bahnk*
the currency exchange office	**kantor** *kahn•tohr*
When does the bank open/close?	**O której otwierają/zamykają bank?** *oh ktoo•rehy oht•fyeh•rah•yohm/zah•myh•kah•yohm bahnk*
I'd like to change dollars/pounds into zlotys.	**Chciałbym m /Chciałabym f wymienić dolary/ funty na złotówki.** *hch'yahw•byhm/ hch'yah•wah•byhm vyh•myeh•n'eech' do•lah•ryh/ foon•tyh nah zwoh•toof•kee*
I want to cash some travelers checks.	**Chcę zrealizować czeki podróżne.** *htsèh zreh•ah•lee•zoh•vahch' cheh•kee pohd•roozh•neh*

Prices in Poland generally include **VAT** (sales tax). The price you will pay is the price provided on the sales tag.

At the Bank

I'd like to change money.	**Chciałbym** *m* /**Chciałabym** *f* **wymienić pieniądze.** *hch'yahw·byhm/hch'yah·wah·byhm vyh·myeh·n'eech' pyeh·n'yohn·dzeh*
What's the exchange rate?	**Jaki jest kurs wymiany?** *yah·kee yehst koors vyh·myah·nyh*
How much is the fee?	**Jaka jest prowizja?** *yah·kah yest proh·veez·yah*
I've lost my travelers checks/ credit cards.	**Zgubiłem** *m* /**Zgubiłam** *f* **czeki podróżne/karty kredytowe.** *zgoo·bee·wehm/zgoo·bee·wahm cheh·kee pohd·roozh·neh/kahr·tyh kreh·dyh·toh·veh*
My card was stolen.	**Ukradli mi kartę.** *oo·krahd·lee mee kahr·teh*
My card doesn't work.	**Moja karta nie działa.** *moh·yah kahr·tah n'yeh dj'yah·wah*

For Numbers, see page 171.

YOU MAY SEE...

Polish currency is currently the **złoty**; one **złoty** is made up of 100 **groszy**. Soon Poland may adopt the euro as its national currency; until then **złoty** is the accepted form of payment.
Coins: 1, 2, 5, 10, 20, 50 **groszy**; 1, 2, 5 **złoty**.
Bills: 10, 20, 50, 100, 200 **złoty**.

YOU MAY SEE...

WŁÓŻ KARTĘ	insert credit card
WYBIERZ JĘZYK	select language
WPROWADŹ PIN	enter your PIN
WCIŚNIJ KLAWISZ	press key
WYPŁATA GOTÓWKI	cash withdrawal
INNA KWOTA	different amount
STAN RACHUNKU	balance inquiry
WOLNE ŚRODKI	available balance
AKCEPTUJ	enter
ANULUJ	cancel
POPRAW	clear
KONTYNUUJ	next
KONIEC	end
POTWIERDZENIE	receipt

Banks are usually open between 8:00 a.m. and 6:00 p.m. When changing cash and travelers checks, you will need to show your passport. Numerous **kantory** (currency exchange offices) provide exchange services and usually have a better exchange rate than banks. Some large hotels will exchange cash and travelers checks for their guests. In cities and larger towns you'll find **bankomaty**, ATMs that accept various international bank and credit cards. Travelers checks are not currently accepted in stores and hotels.

Getting Around

ESSENTIAL

How do I get to town?	**Jak stąd dojechać do miasta?** *yahk stohnt doh•yeh•hahch' doh myahs•tah*
Where's...?	**Gdzie jest...?** *gdj'yeh yehst...*
the airport	*lotnisko loht•n'ees•koh*
the train [railway] station	**dworzec kolejowy** *dvoh•zhehts koh•leh•yoh•vyh*
the bus station	**dworzec autobusowy** *dvoh•zhehts ahw•toh•boo•soh•vyh*
the metro [underground] station	**stacja metra** *stahts•yah meht•rah*
Is it far from here?	**Czy to daleko stąd?** *chyh toh dah•leh•koh stohnt*
Where can I buy tickets?	**Gdzie mogę kupić bilety?** *gdj'yeh moh•geh koo•peech' bee•leh•tyh*
A one-way [single]/ round-trip [return] ticket to...	**Bilet w jedną stonę/powrotny do...** *bee•leht vyehd•nohm stroh•neh/pohv•roht•nyh doh...*
Are there any discounts?	**Czy są jakieś zniżki?** *chyh sohm yah•kyehsh' zn'eesh•kee*
Where can I get a taxi?	**Gdzie mogę złapać taksówkę?** *gdj'yeh moh•geh zwah•pahch' tahk•soof•keh*
Please take me to this address.	**Proszę mnie zawieźć pod ten adres.** *proh•sheh mn'yeh zah•vyehsh'ch' poht tehn ahd•rehs*
Where can I rent a car?	**Gdzie mogę wynająć samochód?** *gdj'yeh moh•geh vyh•nah•yohn'ch' sah•moh•hoot*
Can I have a map, please?	**Poproszę mapę.** *poh•proh•sheh mah•peh*

Tickets

When's…to Cracow?	**O której jest…do Krakowa?** *oh ktoo·rehy yehst… doh krah·koh·vah*	
the (first) bus	**(pierwszy) autobus** *(pyehr·shyh) ahw·toh·boos*	
the (next) flight	**(następny) samolot** *(nahs·tehm·pnyh) sah·moh·loht*	
the (last) train	**(ostatni) pociąg** *(ohs·taht·n'ee) poh·ch'yonk*	
Where can I buy a ticket?	**Gdzie mogę kupić bilet?** *gdj'yeh moh·geh koo·peech' bee·leht*	
One/two ticket(s), please.	**Jeden bilet/Dwa bilety proszę.** *yeh·dehn bee·leht/ dvah bee·leh·tyh proh·sheh*	
A…ticket.	**Bilet…** *bee·leht…*	
one-way [single]	**w jedną stronę** *vyehd·nohm stroh·neh*	
round-trip [return]	**powrotny** *pohv·roht·nyh*	
first class	**w pierwszej klasie** *fpyehr·shehy klah·sh'yeh*	
economy class	**w klasie turystycznej** *fklah·sh'yeh too·ryhs·tyhch·nehy*	
How much?	**Ile to kosztuje?** *ee·leh toh kohsh·too·yeh*	
Is there a discount for…?	**Czy jest zniżka dla…?** *chyh yehst zn'eesh·kah dlah…*	
children	**dzieci** *dj'ye·ch'ee*	
students	**studentów** *stoo·dehn·toof*	
senior citizens	**emerytów** *eh·meh·ryh·toof*	

I have an e-ticket.	**Mam bilet elektroniczny.** *mahm bee·leht eh·lehk·troh·n'eech·nyh*
Can I buy a ticket on the bus/train?	**Czy można kupić bilet w autobusie/pociągu?** *chyh mohzh·nah koo·peech' bee·leht v ahw·toh·boo·sh'yeh/poh·ch'yohn·goo*
I'd like to...my reservation.	**Chciałbym m /Chciałabym f...moją rezerwację.** *hch'yahw·byhm/hch'yah·wah·byhm...moh·yohm reh·zehr·vahts·yeh*
cancel	**odwołać** *ohd·voh·wahch'*
change	**zmienić** *zmyeh·n'eech'*
confirm	**potwierdzić** *poh·tfyehr·dj'eech'*

Plane

Airport Transfer

How much is a taxi to the airport?	**Ile kosztuje taksówka na lotnisko?** *ee·leh kohsh·too·yeh tahk·soof·kah nah loht·n'ees·koh*
To...Airport, please.	**Na lotnisko...proszę.** *nah loht·n'ees·koh...proh·sheh*
My airline is...	**Lecę liniami...** *leh·tseh lee·n'yah·mee...*
My flight leaves at...	**Mam samolot o...** *mahm sah·moh·loht oh...*
I'm in a hurry.	**Spieszę się.** *spyeh·sheh sh'yeh*
Can you drive faster/slower?	**Mógłby pan jechać szybciej/wolniej?** *moogw·byh pahn yeh·hahch' shyhp·ch'yehy/vohl·n'yehy*

For Time, see page 173.

YOU MAY HEAR...

Jakimi liniami pan leci? *yah·kee·mee lee·n'yah·mee pahn leh·ch'ee*	What airline are you flying?
Lot krajowy czy zagraniczny? *loht krah·yoh·wyh chyh zah·grah·n'eech·nyh*	Domestic or international flight?
Który terminal? *ktoo·ryh tehr·mee·nahl*	What terminal?

YOU MAY SEE...

PRZYLOTY	arrivals
ODLOTY	departures
ODBIÓR BAGAŻU	baggage claim
ODLOTY KRAJOWE	domestic flights
ODLOTY MIĘDZYNARODOWE	international flights
STANOWISKO ODPRAWY	check-in
WYJŚCIA	departure gates
NIC DO OCLENIA	nothing to declare
TOWARY DO OCLENIA	goods to declare
INFORMACJA CELNA	customs information
WOLNY OBSZAR CELNY	duty-free zone

Checking In

Where's check-in?	**Gdzie jest stanowisko odprawy?** *gdj'yeh yehst stah•noh•vees•koh oht•prah•vyh*
My name is…	**Nazywam się…** *nah•zyh•vahm sh'yeh…*
I'm going to…	**Lecę do…** *leh•tseh doh…*
How much luggage is allowed?	**Ile bagażu mogę wziąć?** *ee•leh bah•gah•zhoo moh•geh wzh'yohn'ch'*
Which terminal does flight…leave from?	**Z którego terminalu odlatuje lot numer…?** *sktoo•reh•goh tehr•mee•nah•loo ohd•lah•too•yeh loht noo•mehr…*
Which gate does flight…leave from?	**Które wyjście jest dla lotu numer…?** *ktoo•reh vyhy•sh'ch'yeh yehst dlah loh•too noo•mehr…*
I'd like a window/ an aisle seat.	**Chciałbym** *m* **/Chciałabym** *f* **miejsce przy oknie/ przejściu.** *hch'yahw•byhm/hch'yah•wah•byhm myehys•tseh pshyh ohk•n'yeh/pshehy•sh'ch'yoo*

Can I take this on board?	**Czy mogę to wziąć jako bagaż podręczny?** *chyh moh·geh toh vzh'yohn'ch' yah·koh bah·gahsh pohd·rehn·chnyh*
When do we leave/ arrive?	**O której startujemy/lądujemy?** *oh ktoo·rehy stahr·too·yeh·myh/lohn·doo·yeh·myh*
Is flight...delayed?	**Czy lot...jest opóźniony?** *chyh loht...yehst oh·poozh'·n'yoh·nyh*
How late will it be?	**O ile jest opóźniony?** *oh ee·leh yehst oh·poozh'·n'yoh·nyh*

YOU MAY HEAR...

Proszę następną osobę! *proh·sheh nah·stehmp·nohm oh·soh·beh*
Next person, please!

Poproszę paszport/bilet. *poh·proh·sheh pahsh·pohrt/bee·leht*
Your passport/ticket, please.

Ma pan jakiś bagaż do nadania? *mah pahn yah·keesh' bah·gahsh doh nah·dah·n'yah*
Are you checking in any luggage?

Ma pan nadbagaż. *mah pahn nahd·bah·gash*
You have excess luggage.

Czy pan się sam pakował? *chyh pahn sh'yeh sahm pah·koh·vahw*
Did you pack these bags yourself?

Proszę opróżnić kieszenie. *proh·sheh ohp·roozh·n'eech' kyeh·sheh·n'yeh*
Please empty your pockets.

Proszę zdjąć buty. *proh·sheh zdyohn'ch' boo·tyh*
Please take off your shoes.

Zapraszamy pasażerów na pokład samolotu do..., rejs numer... *zah·prah·shah·myh pah·sah·zheh·roov nah pohk·wahd sah·moh·loh·too doh...rehys noo·mehr...*
Now boarding flight number...to...

Luggage

Where is/are...?	**Gdzie jest/są...?** *gdj'yeh yehst/sohm...*
the luggage carts [trolleys]	**wózki bagażowe** *voos-kee bah-gah-zhoh-veh*
luggage lockers/ baggage room	**skrytki bagażowe/przechowalnia bagażu** *skryht-kee bah-gah-zhoh-veh/psheh-hoh-vahl-n'yah bah-gah-zhoo*
the baggage claim	**odbiór bagażu** *ohd-byoor bah-gah-zhoo*
My luggage has been lost.	**Zgubili mój bagaż.** *zgoo-bee-lee mooy bah-gahsh*
My baggage has been stolen.	**Ukradli mi bagaż.** *oo-krahd-lee mee bah-gahsh*
My suitcase was damaged.	**Moja walizka została uszkodzona.** *moh-yah vah-lees-kah zohs-tah-wah oosh-koh-dzoh-nah*

Finding your Way

Where is/are...?	**Gdzie jest/są...?** *gdj'yeh yehst/sohm...*
the currency exchange office	**kantor** *kahn-tohr*
the exit	**wyjście** *vyhsh'ch'yeh*
the taxis	**taksówki** *tahk-soof-kee*
Where is the car rental [hire]?	**Gdzie można wynająć samochód?** *gdj'yeh mohzh-nah wyh-nah-yohn'ch' sah-moh-hoot*
Is there...into town?	**Czy można stąd dojechać...do centrum?** *chyh mohzh-nah stohnt doh-yeh-hahch'...doh tsehn-troom*
a bus	**autobusem** *ahw-toh-boo-sehm*
a train	**pociągiem** *poh-ch'yohn-gyehm*
a metro	**metrem** *meht-rehm*

For Asking Directions, see page 34.

Train

Where's the train station?	**Gdzie jest dworzec kolejowy?** _gdj'yeh yehst dvoh·zhehts koh·leh·yoh·vyh_
Is it far from here?	**Czy to daleko stąd?** _chyh toh dah·leh·koh stohnt_
Where is/are...?	**Gdzie jest/są...?** _gdj'yeh yehst/sohm..._
the ticket office	**kasa biletowa** _kah·sah bee·leh·toh·vah_

Poland has a well-developed train network operated by state-owned **PKP (Polskie Koleje Państwowe)** and some regional operators (e.g. **Tanie Linie Kolejowe, TLK**, and **Koleje Mazowieckie, KM**). Train travel within Poland is relatively cheap. Fares differ according to the route, type of train and seating class you select. Trains that require seat reservations display the letter **R** on both the schedule and the car. You can buy tickets at the train station's ticket office or at an Orbis travel agency. It is also possible to buy tickets on the train for an additional fee. Tickets for **InterCity,** express trains and **TLK** trains are also available on the internet (www.pkp.pl). If you need a reservation, your ticket will be automatically sold with **miejscówka**, the reservation component, subject to extra charge.

YOU MAY SEE...

PERONY	platforms
INFORMACJA	information
REZERWACJE	reservations
PRZYJAZDY	arrivals
ODJAZDY	departures
KASA BILETOWA (CZYNNA/ NIECZYNNA)	ticket office (open/closed)
ROZKŁAD JAZDY	schedule [timetable]
WYJŚCIE (EWAKUACYJNE)	(emergency) exit
TOALETY	restroom [toilet]
POSTÓJ TAKSÓWEK	taxi stand
BIURO RZECZY ZNALEZIONYCH	lost-and-found [lost property office]

the information desk	**informacja** *een·fohr·mah·tsyah*
luggage lockers/ baggage room	**skrytki bagażowe/przechowalnia bagażu** *skryht·kee bah·gah·zhoh·veh/psheh·hoh·vahl·n'yah bah·gah·zhoo*
the platforms	**perony** *peh·roh·nyh*
Can I have a schedule [timetable]?	**Czy mogę prosić rozkład jazdy?** *chyh moh·geh proh·sh'eech' rohs·kwaht yahz·dyh*
How long is the trip [journey]?	**Jak długo trwa podróż?** *yahk dwoo·goh trfah poh·droosh*
Do I have to change trains?	**Czy muszę się przesiadać?** *chyh moo·sheh sh'yeh psheh·sh'yah·dahch'*
Do I need a reservation for this train?	**Muszę kupować miejscówkę?** *moo·sheh koo·poh·vahch' myehys·tsoof·keh*

For Asking Directions, see page 34.

For Tickets, see page 19.

Departures

Which track [platform] does the train to... leave from?	**Z którego toru [peronu] odjeżdża pociąg do...?** *sktoo-reh-goh toh-roo [peh-roh-noo] ohd-yehzh-djah poh-ch'yohnk doh...*
Is this the right track [platform] for...?	**Czy to z tego toru [peronu] odjeżdża pociąg do...?** *chyh toh steh-goh toh-roo [peh-roh-noo] ohd-yehzh-djah poh-ch'yohnk doh...*
Where is track [platform]...?	**Gdzie jest tor [peron]...?** *gdj'yeh yehst tohr [peh-rohn]...*
Where do I change for...?	**Gdzie mam się przesiąść na pociąg do...?** *gdj'yeh mahm sh'yeh psheh-sh'yohn'sh'ch' nah poh-ch'yonk doh...*

On Board

Is this seat free?	**Czy to miejsce jest wolne?** *chyh toh mychys-tsch yehst vohl-neh*
That's my seat.	**To moje miejsce.** *toh moh-yeh myehys-tseh*

Bus

Where's the bus station?	**Gdzie jest dworzec autobusowy?** *gdj'yeh yehst dvoh-zhehts ahw-toh-boo-soh-vyh*

YOU MAY HEAR...

Proszę wsiadać! *proh-sheh fsh'yah-dahch'*	All aboard!
Proszę bilety do kontroli. *proh-sheh bee-leh-tyh doh kohn-troh-lee*	Tickets, please.
Następna stacja... *nahs-tehmp-nah stahts-yah...*	Next stop...
Musi pan się przesiąść w... *moo-sh'ee pahn sh'yeh psheh-sh'yohn'sh'ch' v...*	You have to change at...

Bus service in Poland is extensive. **PKS (Przedsiębiorstwo Komunikacji Samochodowej)** offers the widest range of routes; **Polski Express** also has numerous national routes. You can buy tickets for **PKS** buses at the bus station ticket office or from the driver. Tickets for **Polski Express** buses can be bought at bus stations or at special ticket offices in towns.

Is it far from here?	**Czy to daleko stąd?** *chyh toh dah•leh•koh stohnt*
How do I get to…?	**Jak dojechać do…?** *yahk doh•yeh•hahch' doh…*
Does this bus stop at…?	**Czy ten autobus zatrzymuje się w…?** *chyh tehn ahw•toh•boos zah•tshyh•moo•yeh sh'yeh v…*
Could you tell me when to get off?	**Czy może mi pan powiedzieć, kiedy wysiąść?** *chyh moh•zhe mee pahn poh•vyeh•dj'yehch' kyeh•dyh vyh•sh'on'sh'ch'*
Do I have to change buses?	**Czy muszę się przesiadać?** *chyh moo•sheh sh'yeh psheh•sh'yah•dahch'*
Stop here, please!	**Proszę się zatrzymać!** *proh•sheh sh'yeh zaht•shyh•mahch'*

For Tickets, see page 19.

YOU MAY SEE…

PRZYSTANEK AUTOBUSOWY	bus stop
OTWIERANIE DRZWI PRZYCISKIEM	press to open door
SKASUJ BILET	validate your ticket
HAMULEC BEZPIECZEŃSTWA	emergency brake
KASOWNIK	validation machine
WYJŚCIE AWARYJNE	emergency exit

Warsaw is the only Polish city with a metro service. The line passes through **Centrum** (the city center), where visitors can admire **Pałac Kultury i Nauki** (Palace of Culture and Science). Maps are located throughout metro stations and inside trains. Above-ground **tramwaje** (trams) can be found in Warsaw, Gdańsk, Poznań and many other cities.

Metro

Where's the nearest metro [underground] station?	**Gdzie jest najbliższa stacja metra?** gdj'yeh yehst nahy·bleesh·shah stahts·yah meht·rah
Where can I find a metro map?	**Gdzie mogę znaleźć mapę metra?** gdj'yeh moh·geh znah·lesh'ch' mah·peh meht·rah
Which metro goes in the direction of…?	**Które metro jedzie w stronę…?** ktoo·reh meht·roh yeh·dj'yeh fstroh·neh…
Do I have to transfer [change]?	**Czy muszę się przesiadać?** chyh moo·sheh sh'yeh psheh·sh'yah·dahch'
Is this the metro / train to…?	**Czy to metro jedzie do…?** chyh toh meht·roh yeh·dj'yeh doh…
Where are we?	**Gdzie jesteśmy?** gdj'yeh yehs·tehsh'·myh

For Tickets, see page 19.

Boat & Ferry

When is the ferry to…?	**Kiedy odpływa prom do…?** kyeh·dyh oht·pwyh·vah prohm doh…
Can I take my car?	**Czy mogę zabrać na pokład mój samochód?** chyh moh·geh zahb·rahch' nah pohk·wahd mooy sah·moh·hoot
What time is the next sailing?	**O której jest następny rejs?** oh ktoo·rehy yehst nahs·tehm·pnyh reyhs

Tickets for the metro and trams should be bought before boarding from kiosks or local shops. On boarding you must validate your ticket in a **kasownik** (validation machine). Unvalidated tickets result in an on-the-spot fine. Different types of tickets are used in different cities, but usually single-trip tickets and multiple-trip travelcards are available. In some cities electronic cards are available as well.

YOU MAY SEE...

ŁODZIE RATUNKOWE	life boats
KAPOKI	life jackets
POKŁAD	deck

Can I book a seat/cabin?	**Chciałbym m / Chciałabym f zarezerwować miejsce siedzące/kabinę.** *hch'yahw•byhm/ hch'yah•wah•byhm zah•reh•zehr•voh•vach' myehys•tseh sh'yeh•dzohn•tse/kah•bee•neh*
How long is the crossing?	**Jak długo trwa przeprawa?** *yahk dwoo•goh trfah psheh•prah•vah*

For Tickets, see page 19.

Regular ferry services to and from Denmark and Sweden operate from Świnoujście, Gdańsk and Gdynia. There are several ferry operators who offer various cruises on the Baltic Sea on different days of the week.

Taxi

Where can I get a taxi?	**Gdzie mogę złapać taksówkę?** *gdj'yeh moh•geh zwah•pahch' tahk•soof•keh*
I'd like a taxi now/for tomorrow at…	**Chciałbym** *m* **/Chciałabym** *f* **zamówić taksówkę na jak najszybciej/na jutro na godzinę…** *hch'yahw•byhm/hch'yah•wah•byhm zah•moo•veech' tahk•soof•keh nah yahk nahy•shyhp•ch'yehy/nah yoot•roh nah goh•dj'ee•neh…*
The pick-up address is…	**Proszę mnie odebrać z…** *proh•sheh mn'yeh oh•dehb•rahch' z…*
I'm going to…	**Proszę…** *proh•sheh…*
this address	**pod ten adres** *poht tehn ahd•rehs*
the airport	**na lotnisko** *nah loht•n'ees•koh*
the train station	**na dworzec kolejowy** *nah dvoh•zhehts koh•leh•yoh•vyh*
How much?	**Ile płacę?** *ee•leh pwah•tseh*

YOU MAY HEAR…

Dokąd jedziemy? *doh•kohnt yeh•dj'yeh•myh*	Where to?
Jaki adres? *yah•kee ahd•rehs*	What's the address?

Schedule a taxi pick up by calling a local company; check the phone book for listings. You may be able to hail a taxi but make sure it displays a recognized taxi company name and that the meter is started. A table of fares should be displayed in the taxi. Fares are higher on Sundays, public holidays and at night. Be careful about taking a taxi to suburbs of the city, as it may mean entering another fare zone. Most taxis take cash only. It is not customary to tip the taxi drivers.

I'm late.	**Jestem spóźniony** *m* **/spóźniona** *f*. _yehs_•tehm spoozh'•n'yoh•nyh/spoozh'•n'yoh•nah
Can you drive faster/ slower?	**Mógłby pan jechać szybciej/wolniej?** _moogw_•byh pahn _yeh_•hahch' shyhp•ch'yehy/_vohl_•n'yey
Stop/Wait here, please.	**Proszę się tu zatrzymać/tu zaczekać.** _proh_•sheh sh'yeh too zaht•_shyh_•mahch'/too zah•_cheh_•kahch'
You said it would cost...	**Mówił pan, że to będzie kosztowało...** _moo_•veew pahn zheh toh _behn'_•dj'yeh kohsh•toh•_vah_•woh...
Keep the change.	**Proszę zatrzymać resztę.** _proh_•sheh zah•_tshyh_•mahch' _rehsh_•teh

Bicycle & Motorbike

I'd like to rent...	**Chciałbym** *m* **/Chciałabym** *f* **wynająć...** _hch'yahw_•byhm/hch'yah•wah•byhm vyh•_nah_•yohnch'...
a bicycle	**rower** _roh_•vehr
a moped	**motorower** moh•toh•_roh_•vehr
a motorcycle	**motor** _moh_•tohr
How much per day/ week?	**Ile kosztuje wynajęcie na dzień/tydzień?** _ee_•leh kohsh•_too_•yeh vyh•nah•_yehn'_•ch'yeh nah dj'yehn'/ _tyh_•dj'yehn'

Poproszę prawo jazdy. poh·*proh*·sheh *prah*·voh *yah*·zdyh — Your driver's license, please.

Poproszę paszport. poh·*proh*·sheh pahsh·pohrt — Your passport, please.

Proszę tutaj podpisać. *proh*·sheh too·tahy poht·*pee*·sahch' — Please sign here.

Can I have a helmet/lock?	**Mogę prosić kask/blokadę?** *moh*·geh *proh*·sh'eech' kahsk/bloh·*kah*·deh

Car Hire

Where can I rent a car?	**Gdzie mogę wynająć samochód?** gdj'yeh *moh*·geh vyh·*nah*·yohn'ch' sah·*moh*·hoot
I'd like to rent...	**Chcę wynająć...** htseh vyh·*nah*·yohn'ch'...
an automatic/ a manual	**samochód z automatyczną/ręczną skrzynią biegów** sah·*moh*·hoot z ahw·toh·mah·*tyhch*·nohm/ *rehnch*·nohm skshyh·n'yohm *byeh*·goof
a car with air conditioning	**samochód z klimatyzacją** sah·*moh*·hoot sklee·mah·tyh·*zahts*·yohm
a car seat	**fotelik dziecięcy** foh·*teh*·leek dj'yeh·*ch'yehn*·tsyh
How much...?	**Ile to kosztuje...?** *ee*·leh toh kohsh·*too*·yeh...
per day/week	**za dzień/tydzień** zah dj'yehn'/tyh·dj'yehn'
per kilometer	**za kilometr** zah kee·*loh*·mehtr

Pb 95	regular
Pb 98	premium [super]
ON	diesel
LPG	autogas

for unlimited mileage	**bez limitu kilometrów** *behs lee·mee·too kee·loh·meht·roof*
with insurance	**z ubezpieczeniem** *zoo·behs·pyeh·cheh·n'yehm*
Are there any discounts?	**Czy są jakieś zniżki?** *chyh sohm yah·kyehsh' zn'eezh·kee*

Fuel Station

Where's the next gas [petrol] station?	**Gdzie jest najbliższa stacja benzynowa?** *gdj'yeh yehst nahy·bleesh·shah stah·tsyah behn·zyh·noh·vah*
Fill it up, please.	**Do pełna, proszę.** *doh pehw·nah proh·sheh*
. . .liters, please.	**. . .litrów, proszę.** *. . .leet·roof proh·sheh*
I'll pay in cash/ by credit card.	**Zapłacę gotówką/kartą kredytową.** *zap·wah·tseh goh·toof·kohm/kahr·tohm kreh·dyh·toh·vohm*

For Numbers, see page 171.

YOU MAY HEAR...

Proszę jechać... *proh·sheh yeh·hahch'. . .*	You should go...
prosto *prohs·toh*	straight
w lewo *vleh·voh*	left
w prawo *fprah·voh*	right
na północ/południe *nah poow·nohts/ poh·wood·n'yeh*	north/south
na wschód/zachód *na fs·hoot/zah·hoot*	east/west
To jest... *toh yehst. . .*	It's...
na rogu/za rogiem *nah roh·goo/ zah roh·gyehm*	on/around the corner
naprzeciwko... *nah psheh·ch'eef·koh. . .*	opposite...
za... *zah. . .*	behind...
przy... *pshyh. . .*	next to...

YOU MAY SEE...

	DROGA JEDNOKIERUNKOWA	one way
	DROGA Z PIERWSZEŃSTWEM	right of way
	PRZEJŚCIE DLA PIESZYCH	pedestrian crossing
STOP	**STOP**	stop
	ZAKAZ PARKOWANIA	no parking
	ZAKAZ WJAZDU	no entry
	ZAKAZ WYPRZEDZANIA	passing prohibited
	ZAKAZ ZAWRACANIA	no U-turn

Asking Directions

Is this the right road to...?	**Czy to właściwa droga do...?** *chyh toh vwahsh'·ch'ee·vah droh·gah doh...*
How far is it to...?	**Jak daleko jest stąd do...?** *yahk dah·leh·koh yehst stohnt doh...*
Where's...?	**Gdzie jest...?** *gdj'yeh yehst...*
...Street	**ulica...** *oo·lee·tsah...*
this address	**ten adres** *tehn ahd·rehs*
the highway [motorway]	**autostrada** *ahw·toh·strah·dah*

| Can you show me on the map? | **Czy może mi pan pokazać na mapie?** *chyh moh•zheh mee pahn poh•kah•zahch' nah mah•pyeh* |
| I'm lost. | **Zgubiłem m /Zgubiłam f się.** *zgoo•bee•wehm/ zgoo•bee•wahm sh'yeh* |

Parking

Can I park here?	**Czy mogę tu zaparkować?** *chyh moh•geh too zah•pahr•koh•vahch'*
Where is the nearest parking lot [car park]?	**Gdzie jest najbliższy parking?** *gdj'yeh yehst nahy•bleesh•shyh pahr•keenk*
How much…?	**Ile kosztuje…?** *ee•leh kohsh•too•yeh…*
per hour	**godzina** *goh•dj'ee•nah*
per day	**dzień** *dj'yehn'*
for overnight	**zostawienie samochodu na noc** *zohs•tah•vyeh•n'yeh sah•moh•hoh•doo nah nohts*

Breakdown & Repair

My car broke down/ won't start.	**Mój samochód się zepsuł/nie chce zapalić.** *mooy sah•moh•hoot sh'yeh zehp•soow/n'yeh htseh zah•pah•leech'*
Can you fix it (today)?	**Możecie to naprawić (dzisiaj)?** *moh•zheh•ch'yeh toh nahp•rah•veech' (dj'ee•sh'yahy)*
When can I pick up the car?	**Kiedy mogę odebrać samochód?** *kyeh•dyh moh•geh oh•dehb•rahch' sah•moh•hoot*
How much?	**Ile to kosztuje?** *ee•leh toh kohsh•too•yeh*

Accidents

| There was an accident. | **Był wypadek.** *byhw vyh•pah•dehk* |
| Call an ambulance/ the police. | **Proszę wezwać karetkę/policję.** *proh•sheh vehz•vahch' kah•reht•keh/poh•leets•yeh* |

Places to Stay

ESSENTIAL

Can you recommend a hotel?	**Czy może mi pan polecić jakiś hotel?** *chyh moh·zheh mee pahn poh·leh·ch'eech' yah·keesh' hoh·tehl*
I have a reservation.	**Mam rezerwację.** *mahm reh·zehr·vahts·yeh*
My name is...	**Nazywam się...** *nah·zyh·vahm sh'yeh...*
I would like a room...	**Chciałbym m /Chciałabym f wynająć pokój...** *hch'yahw·byhm/hch'yah·wah·byhm vyh·nah·yohn'ch' poh·kooy...*
for one/two	**jednoosobowy/dwuosobowy** *yehd·noh·oh·soh·boh·vyh/dvoo·oh·soh·boh·vyh*
with a bathroom	**z łazienką** *zwah·zh'yehn·kohm*
with air conditioning	**z klimatyzacją** *sklee·mah·tyh·zahts·yohm*
For...	**Na...** *nah...*
tonight	**tę noc** *teh nohts*
two nights	**dwie noce** *dvyeh noh·tseh*
one week	**tydzień** *tyh·dj'yehn'*
How much?	**Ile to kosztuje?** *ee·leh toh kohsh·too·yeh*
Do you have anything cheaper?	**Czy są jakieś tańsze pokoje?** *chyh sohm yah·kyehsh' tahn'·sheh poh·koh·yeh*
When's check-out?	**O której mamy zwolnić pokój?** *oh ktoo·rehy mah·myh zvohl·n'eech' poh·kooy*
Can I leave this in the safe?	**Mogę zostawić to w sejfie?** *moh·geh zohs·tah·veech' toh fsehy·fyeh*
Can I leave my luggage?	**Mogę zostawić mój bagaż?** *moh·geh zohs·tah·veech' mooy bah·gahsh*

Can I have the bill/ a receipt?	**Czy mogę prosić o rachunek/pokwitowanie?** *chyh moh-geh pro-sh'eech' oh rah-hoo-nehk/ poh-kfee-toh-vah-n'yeh*
I'll pay in cash/ by credit card.	**Zapłacę gotówką/kartą kredytową.** *zah-pwah-tseh goh-toof-kohm/kahr-tohm kreh-dyh-toh-vohm*

Somewhere to Stay

Can you recommend a hotel?	**Czy może mi pan polecić jakiś hotel?** *chyh moh-zheh mee pahn poh-leh-ch'eech' yah-keesh' hoh-tehl*
What is it near?	**Koło czego on się znajduje?** *koh-woh cheh-goh ohn sh'yeh znahy-doo-yeh*
How do I get there?	**Jak można się tam dostać?** *yahk mohzh-nah sh'yeh tahm dohs-tahch'*

At the Hotel

I have a reservation.	**Mam rezerwację.** *mahm reh-zehr-vahts-yeh*
My name is...	**Nazywam się...** *nah-zyh-vahm sh'yeh...*
I would like a room...	**Chciałbym** *m* **/Chciałabym** *f* **wynająć pokój...** *hch'yahw-byhm/hch'yah-wah-byhm vyh-nah-yohn'ch' poh-kooy...*
with a bathroom	**z łazienką** *zwah-zh'yehn-kohm*
with air conditioning	**z klimatyzacją** *sklee-mah-tyh-zahts-yohm*

If you have nowhere to stay booked on arrival, visit the local **Informacja Turystyczna** (Tourist Information Office) for recommendations on places to stay. These are usually located in the city center and/or near the train station.

There is a wide choice of places to stay; prices vary according to facilities, location and season. Following are some places to stay.

Hotels: As any other country, Poland has numerous hotels catering to leisure and business travelers. In smaller towns you will mainly find lower class hotels.

Hostels: These are inexpensive, and usually offer both private and dormitory-style rooms.

Tourist Houses: **Domy Turysty** (guest houses), ideal for budget travelers, are run by the **PTTK** (Polish Tourist Country Lovers' Society), which also runs **schroniska górskie** (mountain hostels). These are found mainly in the countryside.

There are many **pensjonaty** (boarding houses) and **pokoje gościnne** (rooms in private houses) available in big towns and resorts, some of which can be found on the internet. In some towns you may book a room through certain tourist agencies, such as **Biuro Kwater Prywatnych** or **Agencja Promocji Miasta**. Most pensjonaty provide meals and/or cooking facilities. They can accommodate fewer guests than hotels but offer a friendly and cozy atmosphere.

for smokers/ non-smokers	**dla palących/niepalących**	_dla pah•lohn•tsyhh/ n'yeh•pah•lohn•tsyhh_
For…	**Na…**	_nah…_
tonight	**tę noc**	_teh nohts_
two nights	**dwie noce**	_dvyeh noh•tseh_
one week	**tydzień**	_tyh•dj'yehn'_
Does the hotel have…?	**Czy jest u państwa…?**	_chyh yehst oo pahn's•tfah…_
a computer for guests	**komputer dla gości**	_kohm•poo•tehr dlah gohsh'•ch'ee_

an elevator [a lift]	**winda** _veen•dah_
(wireless) internet	**(bezprzewodowy) internet**
service	_(behs•psheh•voh•doh•vyh) een•tehr•neht_
room service	**room service** _room sehr•vees_
a pool	**basen** _bah•sehn_
a gym	**siłownia** _sh'ee•wohv•n'yah_
Could I have…?	**Czy mógłbym** _m_ **/mogłabym** _f_ **dostać…?** _chyh moogw•byhm/moh•gwah•byhm dohs•tahch'…_
an extra bed	**dodatkowe łóżko** _doh•daht•koh•veh woozh•koh_

YOU MAY HEAR…

Poproszę pana paszport/kartę kredytową. Your passport/credit card,
poh•proh•sheh pah•nah pahsh•pohrt/kahr•teh please.
kreh•dyh•toh•vohm

Proszę wypełnić ten formularz. _proh•sheh_ Please fill out this form.
vyh•pehw•n'eech' tehn fohr•moo•lahsh

Proszę tutaj podpisać. _proh•sheh too•tahy_ Please sign here.
poht•pee•sahch'

| a cot | **rozkładane łóżko** rohs•kwah•*dah*•neh *woozh*•koh |
| a crib [child's cot] | **łóżeczko dziecięce** woo•*zhehch*•koh dj'yeh•*ch'yehn*•tseh |

For Numbers, see page 171.

Price

| How much per night/ week? | **Jaka jest cena za noc/tydzień?** *yah*•kah yehst *tseh*•nah zah nohts/*tyh*•dj'yehn' |
| Does the price include breakfast/sales tax [VAT]? | **Czy w cenę wliczone jest śniadanie/wliczony jest VAT?** chyh f *tseh*•neh vlee•*choh*•neh yehst sh'n'yah•*dah*•n'yeh/vlee•*choh*•nyh yehst vaht |

Preferences

Can I see the room?	**Czy mógłbym** m **/mogłabym** f **zobaczyć ten pokój?** chyh *moogw*•byhm/moh•*gwah*•byhm zoh•*bah*•chyhch' tehn *poh*•kooy
I'd like a...room.	**Chciałbym** m **/Chciałabym** f **... pokój.** *hch'yahw*•byhm/hch'yah•wah•byhm ... *poh*•kooy
better	**lepszy** *lehp*•shyh
bigger	**większy** *vyenh*•kshyh
cheaper	**tańszy** *tahn'*•shyh
quieter	**cichszy** *ch'ee*•hshyh
I'll take it.	**Wezmę ten pokój** *vehz*•meh tehn *poh*•kooy
No, I won't take it.	**Nie, nie chcę tego pokoju** n'yeh, n'yeh htseh *teh*•goh poh•*koh*•yoo

Questions

Where is/are...?	**Gdzie jest/są...?** gdj'eh yehst/sohm...
the bar	**bar** bahr
the bathrooms [toilets]	**toaleta** toh•ah•*leh*•tah
the elevators [lifts]	**windy** *veen*•dyh

Can I have…?	**Czy mogę dostać…?** *chyh moh·geh dohs·tahch'…*
a blanket	**koc** *kohts*
an iron	**żelazko** *zheh·lahs·koh*
a pillow	**poduszkę** *poh·doosh·keh*
soap	**mydło** *myhd·woh*
toilet paper	**papier toaletowy** *pah·pyehr toh·ah·leh·toh·vyh*
a towel	**ręcznik** *rehnch·n'eek*
Do you have an adapter for this?	**Czy ma pan do tego przejściówkę?** *chyh mah pahn doh teh·goh pshehysh'·ch'yoof·keh*
How do I turn on the lights?	**Jak się włącza światło?** *yahk sh'yeh vwohn·chah sh'fyaht·woh*
Please wake me at…	**Proszę mnie obudzić o…** *proh·sheh mn'yeh oh·boo·dj'eech' oh…*
Could I have my things from the safe?	**Mógłbym m /Mogłabym f wyjąć moje rzeczy z sejfu?** *moogw·byhm/moh·gwah·byhm vyh·yohn'ch' moh·yeh zheh·chyh ssehy·foo*
Can I leave this in the safe?	**Czy mogę to zostawić w sejfie?** *chyh moh·geh toh zohs·tah·veech' fsehy·fyeh*
Is there any mail [post] for me?	**Czy są jakieś listy do mnie?** *chyh sohm yah·kyehsh' lees·tyh doh mn'yeh*

YOU MAY SEE...

PCHAĆ/CIĄGNĄĆ	push/pull
TOALETA	bathrooms [toilet]
PRYSZNICE	showers
WINDY	elevators [lifts]
SCHODY	stairs
PRALNIA	laundry
NIE PRZESZKADZAĆ	do not disturb
DRZWI PRZECIWPOŻAROWE	fire door
WYJŚCIE (AWARYJNE)	(emergency) exit
BUDZENIE TELEFONICZNE	wake-up call

Are there any messages for me? **Czy są dla mnie jakieś wiadomości?** *chyh sohm dlah mn'yeh yah·kyehsh' vyah·doh·mosh'·ch'ee*

Do you have a laundry service? **Czy świadczycie Państwo usługę prania odzieży?** *chyh sh'vyaht·chyh·ch'yeh pahn'·stvoh oo·swoo·geh prah·n'yah oh·dj'yeh·zhy*

Problems

There's a problem. **Mam problem.** *mahm prohb·lehm*

I've lost my key. **Zgubiłem** *m* **/Zgubiłam** *f* **klucz.** *zgoo·bee·wehm/ zgoo·bee·wahm klooch*

I've locked the key in my room. **Zatrzasnąłem** *m* **/Zatrzasnęłam** *f* **klucz w pokoju.** *zah·tshahs·noh·wehm/zah·tshahs·neh·wahm klooch fpoh·koh·yoo*

Poland's electricity is 230 volts. You may need a converter and/ or an adapter for your appliance.

The room is dirty.	**Pokój jest brudny.**	*poh·kooy yehst brood·nyh*
There are bugs in my room.	**W moim pokoju są robaki.**	*vmoh·eem poh·koh·yoo sohm roh·bah·kee*
There is no hot water/ toilet paper.	**Nie ma ciepłej wody/papieru toaletowego.**	*n'yeh mah ch'yehp·wey voh·dyh/pah·pyeh·roo toh·ah·leh·toh·veh·goh*
...doesn't work.	**...nie działa.**	*...n'yeh dj'yah·wah*
Can you fix...?	**Mogą państwo naprawić...?**	*moh·gohm pahn's·tfoh nahp·rah·veech'...*
the air conditioning	**klimatyzację**	*klee·mah·tyh·zahts·yeh*
the fan	**wentylator**	*vehn·tyh·lah·tohr*
he heat [heating]	**ogrzewanie**	*oh·gzheh·vah·n'yeh*
the light	**światło**	*sh'fyaht·woh*
the TV	**telewizor**	*teh·leh·vee·zohr*
the toilet	**toaletę**	*toh·ah·leh·teh*
I'd like another room.	**Chciałbym m /Chciałabym f zmienić pokój.**	*hch'yahw·byh /hch'yah·wah·byhm zmyeh·n'eech' poh·kooy*

Checking Out

When's check-out?	**O której mam zwolnić pokój?**	*oh ktoo·rehy mahm zvohl·n'eech' poh·kooy*
Could I leave my bags here until...?	**Czy mogę zostawić tutaj bagaż do...?**	*chyh moh·geh zohs·tah·veech' too·tahy bah·gahsh doh...*
Can I have an itemized bill/a receipt?	**Czy mogę dostać szczegółowy rachunek/ pokwitowanie?**	*chyh moh·geh dohs·tach' shcheh·goo·woh·vyh ra·hoo·nehk/poh·kfee·toh·vah·n'yeh*
I think there's a mistake in this bill.	**Na tym rachunku chyba jest błąd.**	*nah tyhm rah·hoon·koo hyh·bah yehst blohnt*
I'll pay in cash/by credit card.	**Zapłacę gotówką/kartą kredytową.**	*zah·pwah·tseh goh·toof·kohm/kahr·tohm kreh·dyh·toh·vohm*

Renting

I've reserved an apartment/a room.	**Zarezerwowałem** *m* **/Zarezerwowałam** *f* **mieszkanie/pokój.** *zah·reh·zehr·voh·vah·wehm/ zah·reh·zehr·voh·vah·lahm myehsh·kah·n'yeh/poh·kooy*
My name is…	**Nazywam się…** *nah·zyh·vahm sh'yeh…*
Can I have the key/ key card?	**Czy mogę dostać klucz/kartę?** *chyh moh·geh dohs·tahch' klooch/kahr·teh*
Are there…?	**Czy są…?** *chyh sohm…*
dishes [crockery]	**naczynia** *nah·chyh·n'yah*
pillows	**poduszki** *poh·doosh·kee*
Are there…?	**Czy są/jest…?** *chyh sohm/yehst…*
sheets	**pościel** *pohsh'·ch'yehl*
towels	**ręczniki** *rehnch·nee·kee*
kitchen utensils	**sztućce** *shtooch'·tseh*

YOU MAY SEE…

WODA PITNA	potable water
ZAKAZ BIWAKOWANIA	no camping
ZAKAZ ROZPALANIA GRILLA I OGNISK	no fires or barbecues
ZAKAZ WSTĘPU	no trespassing

When do I put out the bins?	**Kiedy wywożą śmieci?** _kyeh·dyh vyh·voh·zhohm sh'myeh·ch'ee_
...is broken.	**...nie działa.** _...n'yeh dj'yah·wah_
How does...work?	**Jak obsługiwać...?** _yahk ohp·swoo·gee·vahch'..._
the air conditioner	**klimatyzator** _klee·mah·tyh·zah·tohr_
the dishwasher	**zmywarkę** _zmyh·vahr·keh_
the freezer	**zamrażarkę** _zahm·rah·zhahr·keh_
the heater	**grzejnik** _gzhehy·n'eek_
the microwave	**mikrofalówkę** _mee·kroh·fah·loof·keh_
the refrigerator	**lodówkę** _loh·doof·keh_
the stove	**kuchenkę** _koo·hehn·keh_
the washing machine	**pralkę** _prahl·keh_

Domestic Items

Could I have...?	**Czy mogę dostać...?** _chyh moh·geh dohs·tahch'..._
an adapter	**przejściówkę** _pshehysh'·ch'yoof·keh_
aluminum [kitchen] foil	**folię aluminiową** _fohl·yeh ah·loo·mee·n'yoh·vohm_
a bottle opener	**otwieracz do butelek** _oht·fyeh·rahch doh boo·teh·lehk_
a broom	**zmiotkę** _zmyoht·keh_
a can opener	**otwieracz do puszek** _oht·fyeh·rahch doh poo·shehk_
a corkscrew	**korkociąg** _kohr·koh·ch'yohnk_
bin bags	**worki na śmieci** _vohr·kee nah sh'myeh·ch'ee_
matches	**zapałki** _zah·pahw·kee_
a mop	**mopa** _moh·pah_
napkins	**serwetki** _sehr·veht·kee_
paper towels	**papierowe ręczniki** _pah·pyeh·roh·veh rehnch·n'ee·kee_
plastic wrap [cling film]	**folię do żywności** _fohl·yeh doh zhyhv·nohsh'·ch'ee_

a plunger	**przepychacz** *psheh·pyh·hahch*
scissors	**nożyczki** *noh·zhyhch·kee*
a vacuum cleaner	**odkurzacz** *oht·koo·zhahch*

At the Hostel

Do you have any places left for tonight?	**Czy są na dzisiaj wolne miejsca?** *chyh sohm nah dj'ee·sh'yahy vohl·neh myehys·tsah*
I would like a single/ double room.	**Chciałbym** m **/Chciałabym** f **pokój jednoosobowy/ dwuosobowy.** *hch'yahw·byhm/hch'yah·wah·byhm poh·kooy yehd·noh·oh·soh·boh·vyh/dvoo·oh·soh·boh·vyh*
Could I have…?	**Czy mógłbym** m **/mogłabym** f **dostać…?** *chyh moogw·byhm/moh·gwah·byhm dohs·tahch'…*
a blanket	**koc** *kohts*
a pillow	**poduszkę** *poh·doosh·keh*
sheets	**pościel** *pohsh'·ch'yehl*
a towel	**ręcznik** *rehnch·n'eek*
Do you have lockers?	**Czy są tu zamykane schowki?** *Chyh sohm too zah·myh·kah·neh s·hohv·kee*
When do you lock up?	**O której zamykają państwo drzwi?** *oh ktoo·rehy zah·myh·kah·yohm pahn'·stfoh djvee*
Do I need a membership card?	**Czy potrzebuję karty członkowskiej** *Chyh poh·tsheh·boo·yeh kahr·tyh chwohn·kohv·skyehy*
Here's my international student card.	**Oto moja międzynarodowa karta studencka** *oh·toh moh·yah myehn·dzyh·nah·roh·doh·vah kahr·tah stoo·dehn·tskah*

Going Camping

| Can I camp here? | **Mogę tutaj rozbić namiot?** *moh·geh too·tahy rohz·beech' nah·myoht* |
| Is there a campsite near here? | **Czy jest tu w pobliżu jakiś camping?** *chyh yehst too fpoh·blee·zhoo yah·keesh' kehm·peenk* |

What is the charge	**Ile kosztuje jedna noc/tydzień?** *ee·leh*
per day/week?	*kohsh·too·yeh yehd·nah nohts/tyh·dj'yehn'*
Are there . . . ?	**Czy są/jest** *chyh sohm/yehst*
electric outlets	**gniazdka elektryczne** *gn'yahs·tkah eh·lehk·tryh·chneh*
showers?	**prysznice?** *pryhsh·n'ee·tseh*
laundry facilities	**pralnia** *prahl·n'yah*
tents for hire	**namioty do wynajęcia** *nah·myoh·tyh doh*
	vyh·nah·yehn·ch'yah

Where can I empty the **Gdzie mogę opróżnić chemiczną toaletę?**
chemical toilet? *gd'yeh moh·geh ohp·roozh·n'eech'*
heh·meech·nohm toh·ah·leh·teh

For Domestic Items, see page 45.
For In the Kitchen, see page 75.

Communications

ESSENTIAL

Is there an internet	**Czy jest tu gdzieś w pobliżu kafejka**
cafe nearby?	**internetowa?** *chyh yehst too gj'yehsh' fpoh·blee·zhoo*
	kah·fehy·kah een·tehr·neh·toh·vah
Can I access the	**Można tu skorzystać z internetu/sprawdzić**
internet/check	**pocztę?** *mohzh·nah too skoh·zhyhs·tahch'*
e-mails?	*zeen·tehr·neh·too/sprahw·dj'eech' pohch·teh*
How much per hour/	**Ile kosztuje godzina/pół godziny?** *ee·leh*
half hour?	*koh·shtoo·yeh goh·dj'ee·nah/poow goh·dj'ee·nyh*
How do I connect/	**Jak mam się połączyć z siecią/zalogować?** *yahk*
log on?	*mahm sh'yeh poh·wohn·chyhch' ssh'yeh·ch'yohm/*
	zah·loh·goh·vahch'

Is there a password?	**Jest jakieś hasło?** *yehst yah·kyehsh' hahs·woh*
A phone card, please.	**Poproszę kartę telefoniczną.** *poh·proh·sheh kahr·teh teh·leh·foh·n'eech·nohm*
Can I have your phone number?	**Czy mogę prosić pana numer telefonu?** *chyh moh·geh proh·sh'eech' pah·nah noo·mehr teh·leh·foh·noo*
Here's my number/ e-mail address.	**To jest mój numer telefonu/adres e-mail.** *toh yehst mooy noo·mehr teh·leh·foh·noo/ ahd·rehs ee·mehyl*
Can you call me please/e-mail me?	**Czy mógłby pan do mnie zadzwonić/napisać do mnie maila?** *chyh moogw·byh pahn doh mn'yeh zahdz·voh·n'eech'/nah·pee·sahch' doh mn'yeh mehy·lah*
Hello. This is…	**Dzień dobry. Mówi…** *dj'yehn' dohb·ryh moo·vee…*
I'd like to speak to…	**Chciałbym** *m* **/Chciałabym** *f* **rozmawiać z…** *hch'yahw·byhm/hch'yah·wah·byhm rohz·mah·vyahch' z…*
Could you repeat that?	**Może pan powtórzyć?** *moh·zheh pahn pohf·too·zhyhch'*
I'll call back later.	**Zadzwonię później.** *zahdz·voh·n'yeh poozh'·n'yehy*
Bye.	**Do widzenia.** *doh vee·dzeh·n'yah*
Where's the post office?	**Gdzie jest poczta?** *Gdj'yeh yehst pohch·tah*
I'd like to send this to…	**Chciałbym** *m* **/Chciałabym** *f* **to wysłać do…** *hch'yahw·byhm/hch'yah·wah·byhm toh vyhs·wahch' doh…*

Image at top of page

Online

Is there an internet cafe nearby?	**Czy jest tu gdzieś w pobliżu kafejka internetowa?** *chyh yehst too gdj'yehsh' fpoh·blee·zhoo kah·fehy·kah een·tehr·neh·toh·vah*
Does it have wireless internet?	**Jest tam bezprzewodowy internet?** *yehst tahm behs·psheh·voh·doh·vyh een·tehr·neht*
What is the WiFi password?	**Jakie jest hasło do sieci WiFi?** *yah·kyeh yehst hahs·woh doh sh'yeh·ch'ee vee phee*
Is the WiFi free?	**Czy korzystanie z WiFi jest bezpłatne?** *chyh koh·zhyh·stah·nyeh z vee phee yehst behs·pwaht·neh*
Do you have bluetooth?	**masz funkcję Bluetooth?** *mahsh foon·ktsyeh bloo·tooth*
How do I turn the computer on/off?	**Jak włączyć/wyłączyć komputer?** *yak vwohn·chych'/wyh·wohn·chych' kohm·poo·tehr*
How much per hour/half hour?	**Ile kosztuje godzina/pół godziny?** *ee·leh kohsh·too·yeh goh·dj'ee·nah/poow goh·dj'ee·nyh*
Can I…?	**Mogę…?** *moh·geh…*
access the internet	**skorzystać z internetu** *skoh·zhyhs·tahch' zeen·tehr·neh·too*
check e-mail	**sprawdzić pocztę** *sprahv·dj'eech' pohch·teh*

print something	**coś wydrukować** tsohsh' vyh•droo•<u>koh</u>•vahch'
access Skype?	**używać Skype'a?** ooh•<u>zhyh</u>•vahch' <u>skahy</u>•pah
plug in/charge my laptop/iPhone/ iPad/BlackBerry?	**podłączyć/naładować laptopa/iPhone'a/ iPada/Blackberry?** pohd•<u>wohn</u>•chych'/ nah•wah•<u>doh</u>•vach' lahp•<u>toh</u>•pah/ahy•<u>foh</u>•nah/ ahy•<u>pah</u>•dah/blahk•<u>beh</u>•ryh
How do I...?	**Jak mam się...?** yahk mahm sh'yeh...
connect/ disconnect	**połączyć z siecią/rozłączyć** poh•<u>wohn</u>•chych' ssh'yeh•ch'yohm/rohz•<u>wohn</u>•chych'
log on/off	**zalogować/wylogować** zah•loh•<u>goh</u>•vahch'/ wyh•loh•<u>goh</u>•vahch'
How do I type this symbol?	**Jak wpisać ten symbol?** yahk <u>fpee</u>•sahch' tehn <u>syhm</u>•bohl

YOU MAY SEE...

ZAMKNIJ	close
USUŃ	delete
E-MAIL	e-mail
ZAKOŃCZ	exit
POMOC	help
KOMUNIKATOR	instant messenger
ZALOGUJ SIĘ	login
ANULUJ	cancel
OTWARTE	open
DRUKUJ	print
ZAPISZ	save
NAZWA UŻYTKOWNIKA	username
HASŁO	password
(BEZPRZEWODOWY) INTERNET	(wireless) internet

What's your e-mail?	**Jaki jest pana adres e-mail?** _yah•kee yehst pah•nah ahd•rehs ee•mehyl_
My e-mail is…	**Mój e-mail to…** _mooy ee•meyhl toh…_
Do you have a scanner?	**Czy jest tu skaner?** _Chyh yehst too skah•nehr_

Social Media

Are you on Facebook/Twitter?	**Masz konto na Facebooku/Twitterze?** _mahsh kohn•toh nah fehys•boo•koo/twee•teh•zheh_
What's your user name?	**Pod jaką nazwą masz konto?** _pohd yah•kohm nahz•vohm mahsh kohn•toh_
I'll add you as a friend.	**Dodam Cię do znajomych.** _doh•dahm ch'yeh doh znah•yoh•myhh_
I'll follow you on Twitter.	**Będę śledził/śledziła twoje wpisy na Twitterze.** _behn•deh sh'leh•'dj'eewh/sh'leh•'dj'ee•wah tfoh•yeh fpee•syh nah twee•teh•zheh_
Are you following…?	**Czy śledzisz wpisy….?** _chyh sh'leh•dj'eesh fpee•syh…_
I'll put the pictures on Facebook/Twitter.	**Wrzucę zdjęcia na Facebooka/Twittera.** _vzhoo•tseh zdyehn•chy'ahh nah fehys•boo•kah/twee•teh•rah_
I'll tag you in the pictures.	**Zaznaczę cię na zdjęciach.** _zah•znah•cheh ch'yeh nah zdyehn•chy'ahh_

Phone

A phone card, please.	**Poproszę kartę telefoniczną.** _poh•proh•sheh kahr•teh teh•leh•foh•n'eech•nohm_
How much?	**Ile to kosztuje?** _ee•leh toh kohsh•too•yeh_
My phone doesn't work here.	**Mój telefon tu nie działa.** _mooy teh•leh•fohn too n'yeh dj'yah•wah_
What's the country code for…?	**Jaki jest numer kierunkowy do…?** _yah•kee yehst noo•mehr kyeh•roon•koh•vyh doh…_

Public phones are card operated. A local or international **karta telefoniczna** (phone card) can be purchased from kiosks or post offices. Be sure to break off the perforated corner before inserting the card into the phone.

What's the number for Information?	**Jaki jest numer do informacji?**	*yah‧kee yehst noo‧mehr doh een‧fohr‧mahts‧yee*
I'd like the number for...	**Proszę o numer telefonu do...**	*proh‧sh'eh oh noo‧mehr teh‧leh‧foh‧noo doh...*
My phone doesn't work here.	**Mój telefon tu nie działa.**	*mooy teh‧leh‧fohn too n'yeh dj'yah‧wah*
What network are you on?	**W jakiej jesteś sieci?**	*vyah‧kyey yehs‧tehsh' sh'yeh‧ch'ee*
Is it 3G?	**Czy jest to sieć 3G?**	*tchyh yehst toh shy'ech' tshyh gyeh*
I have run out of credit/minutes.	**Skończyła mi się karta.**	*skohn'‧chyh‧wah mee sh'yeh kahr‧tah*
Can I buy some credit?	**Czy mogę tu doładować kartę?**	*tchyh moh‧geh tooh doh‧wah‧doh‧vahch' kahr‧teh*
Do you have a phone charger?	**Czy ma Pan *m* / Pani *f* ładowarkę do telefonu?**	*chyh mah pahn/ pahnee wah‧doh‧vahr‧keh doh teh‧leh‧foh‧noo*
Can I have your phone number?	**Czy mogę dostać twój numer telefonu?**	*chyh moh‧geh doh‧stahch' tfooy noo‧mehr teh‧leh ‧foh‧noo*
Here's my number.	**Oto mój numer telefonu.**	*oh‧toh mooy noo‧mehr teh‧leh ‧foh‧noo*
Please call/text me.	**Zadzwoń do mnie/przyślij mi SMS.**	*zah‧dzvohn' doh mnyeh/pshyh‧sh'leey mee ehs‧ehm‧ehs*

| I'll call/text you. | **Zadzwonię do ciebie/wyślę ci SMS.** *zah•dzvoh•n'yeh doh ch'yeh•byeh/vyh•sh'leh ch'ee ehs•ehm•ehs* |

For Numbers, see page 171.

Telephone Etiquette

Hello. This is...	**Dzień dobry. Mówi...** *dj'yen' dohb•ryh moo•vee...*
I'd like to speak to...	**Chciałbym m / Chciałabym f rozmawiać z...** *hch'yahw•byhm/hch'yah•wah•byhm rohz•mah•vyahch' z...*
Extension...	**Wewnętrzny...** *vehv•nehntsh•nyh...*
Speak louder/more slowly, please.	**Proszę mówić głośniej/wolniej.** *proh•sh'eh moo•veech' gwohsh'•n'yehy/vohl•n'yehy*

YOU MAY HEAR...

Halo. *hah•loh*	Hello.
Przepraszam, kto mówi? *psheh•prah•shahm ktoh moo•vee*	Who's calling, please?
Proszę poczekać. *proh•sheh poh•cheh•kahch'*	Please hold.
Przełączę pana. *psheh•wohn•cheh pah•nah*	I'll put you through.
Nie może teraz podejść. *n'yeh moh•zheh teh•rahs poh•deysh'ch'*	He/She can't come to the phone.
Coś przekazać? *tsohsh' psheh•kah•zahch'*	Would you like to leave a message?
Czy może do pana oddzwonić? *chyh moh•zheh doh pah•nah ohd•dzvoh•n'eech'*	Can he/she call you back?
Jaki jest pana numer telefonu? *yah•kee yehst pah•nah noo•mehr teh•leh•foh•noo*	What's your number?

Could you repeat that?	**Mógłby pan powtórzyć?** _moogw•byh pahn pohf•too•zhyhch'_
I'll call back later.	**Zadzwonię później.** _zahdz•voh•n'yeh poozh'•n'yehy_
Bye.	**Do widzenia.** _doh vee•dzeh•n'yah_

Fax

Can I send/receive a fax here?	**Czy mogę stąd wysłać/tu odebrać faks?** _chyh moh•geh stohnt vyhs•wahch'/too oh•dehb•rahch' fahks_
What's the fax number?	**Jaki jest numer faksu?** _yah•kee yehst noo•mehr fahk•soo_
Please fax this to...	**Proszę to przefaksować do...** _proh•sheh toh psheh•fahk•soh•vahch' doh..._

YOU MAY HEAR...

Proszę wypełnić deklarację celną. _proh•sheh vyh•pehw•n'eech' deh•klah•rahts•yeh tsehl•nohm_ Please fill out the customs declaration form.

Jaka jest wartość przesyłki? _yah•kah yehst wahr•tohsh'ch' psheh•syhw•kee_ What's the value of the package?

Co jest w środku? _tsoh yehst fsh'roht•koo_ What's inside?

Poczta (the post office) has locations throughout Poland. It handles mail and provides courier, phone and fax services. Stamps and postcards can be bought at the post office and at some kiosks. Mailboxes are red and display the logo **Poczta Polska**.

Post

Where's the post office/	**Gdzie jest poczta/skrzynka pocztowa?** *gdj'yeh*
mailbox [postbox]?	*yehst pohch·tah/skshyhn·kah pohch·toh·vah*
A stamp for this	**Poproszę znaczek na tę pocztówkę/ten list.**
postcard/letter, please.	*poh·proh·sheh znah·chehk nah teh pohch·toof·keh/ tehn leest*
How much?	**Ile to kosztuje?** *ee·leh toh kohsh·too·yeh*
I want to send this	**Chcę wysłać tę paczkę pocztą lotniczą/**
package by airmail/	**priorytetem.** *htseh vyhs·wahch' teh pahch·keh*
express mail.	*pohch·tohm loht·n'ee·chohm/pryoh·ryh·teh·tehm*
A receipt, please.	**Poproszę paragon.** *poh·proh·sheh pah·rah·gohn*

Food & Drink

ESSENTIAL

Can you recommend a good restaurant/ cafe?	**Czy może mi pan polecić dobrą restaurację/ kawiarnię?** *chyh moh•zheh mee pahn poh•leh•ch'eech' dohb•rohm rehs•tahw•rahts•yeh/ kah•vyahr•n'yeh*
Is there a traditional Polish/an inexpensive restaurant nearby?	**Czy jest tu gdzieś w pobliżu tradycyjna polska/niedroga restauracja?** *chyh yehst too gdj'yehsh' fpoh•blee•zhoo trah•dyh•tsyhy•nah pohls•kah/n'yeh•droh•gah rehs•tahw•rahts•yah*
A table for one/two, please.	**Stolik dla jednej osoby/dwóch osób, proszę.** *stoh•leek dlah yehd•nehy oh•soh•byh/dvooh oh•soop proh•sheh*
Can we sit…?	**Możemy usiąść…?** *moh•zheh•myh oo•sh'yohn'sh'ch'…*
here/there	**tu/tam** *too/tahm*
outside	**na zewnątrz** *nah zehv•nohntsh*
in a non-smoking area	**w części dla niepalących** *fchehn'sh'•ch'ee dlah n'yeh•pah•lohn•tsyhh*
Where are the toilets?	**Gdzie są toalety?** *gdj'yeh sohm toh•ah•leh•tyh*
Can I have a menu?	**Mogę prosić menu?** *moh•geh proh•sh'eech' meh•nee*
What do you recommend?	**Co może pan polecić?** *tsoh moh•zheh pahn poh•leh•ch'eech'*
I'd like…	**Poproszę…** *poh•proh•sheh…*
Some more…, please.	**Poproszę trochę więcej…** *poh•proh•sheh troh•heh vyehn•tsehy…*
Enjoy your meal.	**Smacznego.** *smahch•neh•goh*
The check [bill], please.	**Poproszę rachunek.** *poh•proh•sheh rah•hoo•nehk*

Is service included?	**Czy obsługa jest wliczona w cenę?** *chyh ohp·swoo·gah yehst vlee·choh·nah ftseh·neh*	
Can I pay by credit card?	**Czy mogę zapłacić kartą kredytową?** *chyh moh·geh zah·pwah·ch'eech' kahr·tohm kreh·dyh·toh·vohm*	
Can I have a receipt?	**Czy mogę prosić paragon?** *chyh moh·geh pro·sh'eech' pah·rah·gohn*	
Thank you.	**Dziękuję.** *dj'yehn·koo·yeh*	

Where to Eat

Can you recommend...?	**Czy może pan polecić...?** *chyh moh·zheh pahn poh·leh·ch'eech'...*
a restaurant	**restaurację** *rehs·tahw·rahts·yeh*
a bar	**bar** *bahr*
a cafe	**kawiarnię** *kah·vyahr·n'yeh*
a fast-food place	**fast-food** *fahst·foot*
an ice-cream parlor	**lodziarnię** *loh·dj'yahr·n'yeh*
a pub	**pub** *pahp*
a cheap restaurant	**niedroga restauracja** *n'yeh·droh·gah rehs·tahw·rahts·yah*
an expensive restaurant	**droga restauracja** *droh·gah rehs·tahw·rahts·yah*
a restaurant with a good view	**restauracja z dobrym widokiem** *rehs·tahw·rahts·yah zdohb·ryhm vee·doh·kyehm*
an authentic/a non-touristy restaurant	**tradycyjna restauracja/restauracja lubiana przez miejscowych** *trah·dyh·tsyhy·nah rehs·tahw·rahts·yah / rehs·tahw·rahts·yah loo·byah·nah pshez myehys·tsoh·vyh*

Reservations & Preferences

I'd like to reserve a table...	**Chciałbym** *m* **/Chciałabym** *f* **zarezerwować stolik...** *hch'yahw·byhm/hch'yah·wah·byhm zah·reh·zehr·voh·vahch' stoh·leek...*
for two	**dla dwóch osób** *dlah dvooh oh·soop*
for this evening	**na dziś wieczór** *nah dj'eesh vyeh·choor*
for tomorrow at...	**na jutro na...** *nah yoot·roh nah...*
A table for two, please.	**Proszę stolik dla dwóch osób.** *proh·sheh stoh·leek dlah dvooh oh·soop*
I have a reservation.	**Mam rezerwację.** *mahm reh·zehr·vahts·yeh*
My name is...	**Nazywam się...** *nah·zyh·vahm sh'yeh...*
Can we sit...?	**Możemy usiąść...?** *moh·zheh·myh oo·sh'yohn'sh'ch'...*
here/there	**tu/tam** *too/tahm*
outside	**na zewnątrz** *nah zehv·nohntsh*
in a non-smoking area	**w części dla niepalących** *fchehnsh'·ch'ee dlah n'yeh·pah·lohn·tsyhh*
by the window	**przy oknie** *pshyh ohk·n'yeh*
in the shade	**w cieniu?** *fch'yeh·n'yoo*
in the sun	**w słońcu?** *fswhon'·tsoo*
Where are the toilets?	**Gdzie są toalety?** *gdj'yeh sohm toh·ah·leh·tyh*

YOU MAY HEAR...

Czy ma pan rezerwację? *chyh mah pahn reh·zehr·vahts·yeh*	Do you have a reservation?
Dla ilu osób? *dlah ee·loo oh·soop*	For how many?
Co podać? *tsoh poh·dahch'*	What would you like?
Polecam... *poh·leh·tsahm...*	I recommend...
Smacznego. *smahch·neh·goh*	Enjoy your meal.

How to Order

Excuse me!	**Przepraszam!** *psheh-prah-shahm*
I'm ready to order.	**Chciałbym** *m* **/Chciałabym** *f* **już zamówić.** *hch'yahw-byhm/hch'yah-wah-byhm yoosh zah-moo-veech'*
May I see the wine list?	**Mogę prosić kartę win?** *moh-geh proh-sheech' kahr-teh veen*
I'd like...	**Poproszę...** *poh-proh-sheh...*
a bottle of...	**butelkę...** *boo-tehl-keh...*
a carafe of...	**karafkę...** *kah-rahf-keh...*
a glass of wine	**kieliszek wina** *kyeh-lee-shehk vee-nah*
a glass of water	**szklankę wody** *shklahn-keh voh-dyh*
Can I have a menu?	**Mogę prosić menu?** *moh-geh proh-sh'eech' meh-nee*
Do you have...?	**Czy mają państwo...?** *chyh mah-yohm pahn's-tfoh...*
a menu in English	**menu po angielsku** *meh-nee poh ahn-gyehls-koo*
a fixed-price menu	**zestawy** *zehs-tah-vyh*
a children's menu	**dania dla dzieci** *dah-n'yah dlah dj'yeh-ch'ee*
What do you recommend?	**Co może pan polecić?** *tsoh moh-zheh pahn poh-leh-ch'eech'*
What's this?	**Co to jest?** *tso toh yehst*
What's in it?	**Z czego to jest zrobione?** *scheh-goh toh yehst zroh-byoh-neh*
Is it spicy?	**Czy to jest ostre?** *chyh toh yehst oh-streh*
I'd like...	**Poproszę...** *poh-proh-sheh...*
More...please.	**Poproszę więcej...** *poh-proh-sheh vyehn-tsehy...*
With/Without...please.	**Poproszę z/bez...** *poh-proh-sheh z/behs...*
I can't eat...	**Nie mogę jeść...** *n'yeh moh-geh yehsh'ch'...*
rare	**krwisty** *krfees-tyh*
medium	**średnio wysmażony** *sh'rehd-n'yoh vyhs-mah-zhoh-nyh*

60

well-done	**dobrze wysmażony** _dohb_·zheh vyhs·mah·_zhoh_·nyh
It's to go [take away].	**Na wynos, poproszę.** nah vyh·nohs poh·proh·sheh
For Drinks, see page 76.	

> **YOU MAY SEE…**
>
> | **DANIA DNIA** | menu of the day |
> | **OBSŁUGA (NIE)WLICZONA W CENĘ** | service (not) included |
> | **SZEF KUCHNI POLECA** | specials |

Cooking Methods

baked	**pieczony** _pyeh·choh_·nyh
boiled	**gotowany** _goh·toh·vah_·nyh
braised	**duszony** _doo·shoh_·nyh
breaded	**panierowany** pah·n'yeh·roh·_vah_·nyh
creamed	**starty** _stahr_·tyh
diced	**pokrojony w kostkę** poh·kroh·_yoh_·nyh _fkohs_·tkeh
filleted	**filet** _fee_·leht
fried	**smażony** smah·_zhoh_·nyh
grilled	**grillowany** gree·loh·_vah_·nyh
poached	**z wody** _zvoh_·dyh
roasted	**pieczony** _pyeh·choh_·nyh
sautéed	**smażony sauté** smah·_zhoh_·nyh _soh_·teh
smoked	**wędzony** vehn·_dzoh_·nyh
steamed	**gotowany na parze** goh·toh·_vah_·nyh nah _pah_·zheh
stewed	**duszony** _doo·shoh_·nyh
stuffed	**faszerowany** fah·sheh·roh·vah·nyh

Dietary Requirements

I'm...	**Jestem...** _yehs·tehm..._	
allergic to...	**uczulony na...** _oo·choo·loh·nyh nah..._	
diabetic	**cukrzykiem** _yehs·tehm tsook·shyh·kyehm_	
lactose intolerant.	**Mam nietolerancję laktozy.** _mahm n'yeh·toh·leh·rahn·tsyeh lahk·toh·zyh_	
vegetarian	**wegetarianinem** _m_ **/wegetarianką** _f_ _veh·geh·tahr·yah·nee·nehm/veg·geh·tah·ryahn·kohm_	
vegan	**weganinem** _m_ **/weganką** _f_ _veh·gah·nee·nehm/ veh·gahn·kohm_	
I can't eat...	**Nie mogę jeść...** _n'yeh moh·geh yehsh'ch'..._	
dairy products	**produktów mlecznych** _proh·dook·toof mlehch·nyhh_	
gluten	**glutenu** _gloo·teh·noo_	
nuts	**orzechów** _oh·zheh·hoot_	
pork	**wieprzowiny** _vyehp·shoh·vee·nyh_	
shellfish	**owoców morza** _oh·voh·tsoof moh·zhah_	
spicy food	**pikantnych potraw** _pee·kahnt·nyhh poht·rahf_	
wheat	**pszenicy** _psheh·nee·tsyh_	
Is it halal/kosher?	**Czy to jest halal/koszerne?** _chyh toh yehst hah·lahl/koh·shehr·neh_	
Do you have...?	**Czy mają państwo...?** _chyh mah·yohm pahn's·tfoh..._	
skimmed milk	**mleko odtłuszczone** _mleh·koh ohd·twoosh·choh·neh_	
whole milk	**mleko pełne** _mleh·koh pehw·neh_	
soya milk	**mleko sojowe** _mleh·koh soh·yoh·veh_	

Dining With Children

Do you have children's portions?	**Mają państwo porcje dla dzieci?** _mah·yohm pahn's·tfoh pohr·tsyeh dlah dj'yeh·ch'ee_

62

Can I have a highchair/ child's seat?	**Mógłbym** *m* **/Mogłabym** *f* **dostać wysokie krzesełko/krzesełko dla dziecka?** *moogw•byhm/ moh•gwah•byhm dohs•tahch' vyh•soh•kyeh ksheh•sehw•koh/ksheh•sehw•koh dlah dj'yehts•kah*
Where can I feed/ change the baby?	**Gdzie mogę nakarmić/przewinąć dziecko?** *gdj'yeh moh•geh nah•kahr•meech'/psheh•vee•nohn'ch' dj'yehts•koh*
Can you warm this?	**Może pan to podgrzać?** *moh•zheh pahn toh pohd•gzhahch'*

For Traveling with Children, see page 146.

How to Complain

When will our food be ready?	**Jak długo jeszcze będziemy czekać na nasze zamówienie?** *yahk dwoo•goh yehsh•cheh behn'•dj'yeh•myh cheh•kahch' nah nah•sheh zah•moo•vyeh•n'yeh*
We can't wait any longer.	**Nie możemy dłużej czekać.** *n'yeh moh•zheh•myh dwoo•zhehy cheh•kach'*
We're leaving.	**Wychodzimy.** *vyh•hoh•dj'ee•myh*
I didn't order this.	**Nie zamawiałem** *m* **/zamawiałam** *f* **tego.** *n'yeh zah•mah•vyah•wehm/zah•mah•vyah•wahm teh•goh*
I ordered…	**Zamawiałem** *m* **/Zamawiałam** *f* **…** *zah•mah•vyah•wehm/zah•mah•vyah•wahm…*
I can't eat this.	**Nie mogę tego jeść.** *n'yeh moh•geh teh•goh yehsh'ch'*
This is too…	**To jest za…** *toh yehst zah…*
cold/hot	**zimne/gorące** *zh'eem•neh/goh•rohn•tseh*
salty/spicy	**słone/ostre** *swoh•neh/ohs•treh*
tough/bland	**twarde/mdłe** *tfahr•deh/mdweh*
This isn't fresh.	**To jest nieświeże.** *toh yehst n'yeh•sh'fyeh•zheh*
This is dirty.	**To jest brudne.** *toh yehst brood•neh*

Paying

The check [bill], please.	**Poproszę rachunek.** *poh-proh-sheh rah-hoo-nehk*
Separate checks [bills], please.	**Chcielibyśmy zapłacić osobno.** *hch'yeh-lee-byhsh'-myh zah-pwah-ch'eech' oh-sohb-noh*
It's all together.	**Proszę policzyć wszystko razem.** *proh-sheh poh-lee-chyhch' fshyhst-koh rah-zehm*
Is service included?	**Czy obługa jest wliczona w cenę?** *chyh ohp-swoo-gah yehst vlee-choh-nah ftseh-neh*
What's this amount for?	**Za co jest ta kwota?** *zah tsoh yehst tah kfoh-tah*
I didn't have that.	**Nie jadłem** *m* **/ jadłam** *f* **tego** *n'yeh yahd-wehm/ yahd-wahm teh-goh*
I had…	**Zjadłem** *m* **/ zjadłam** *f* **…** *zyahd-wehm/ zyahd-wahm* …
Can I pay by credit card?	**Można płacić kartą kredytową?** *mohzh-nah pwah-ch'eech' kahr-tohm kreh-deeh-toh-vohm*
Can I have an itemized bill/a receipt?	**Czy mogę dostać szczegółowy rachunek/ pokwitowanie?** *chyh moh-geh dohs-tahch' shcheh-goo-woh-vyh rah-hoo-nehk/ pohk-fee-toh-vah-n'yeh*
That was delicious.	**Bardzo mi smakowało.** *bahr-dzoh mee smah-koh-vah-woh*
I've already paid	**Już zapłaciłem** *m* **/zapłaciłam** *f*. *yoosh zah-pwah-ch'ee-wehm/zah-pwah-ch'ee-wahm*

It is customary to tip your server 10% of the total bill. In more expensive restaurants the head waiter should also be tipped.

Meals & Cooking

Traditional Polish cuisine was influenced by the climate and location of Poland. Many dishes owe much to neighboring Russia, Germany and Hungary. Heavy soup, meat with root and/or pickled vegetables, cabbage, preserved fruit and dry and pickled mushrooms are still popular. So too are dumpling and noodle dishes. Modern Polish cuisine offers imaginative, healthy derivatives of traditional dishes. Salads and healthy snacks are popular, and vegetarian dishes are now common in restaurants.

Breakfast

boczek _boh·chehk_	bacon
bułki _boow·kee_	rolls
chleb _hlehp_	bread
dżem _djehm_	jam
herbata _hehr·bah·tah_	tea
jajecznica _yah·yehch·n'ee·tsah_	scrambled eggs
jajka sadzone _yahy·kah sah·dzoh·neh_	fried eggs

jajko na twardo/miękko _yahy·koh nah tfahr·doh/myehnk·koh_	hard-boiled/soft-boiled egg
jogurt _yoh·goort_	yogurt
kawa _kah·vah_	coffee
marmolada _mahr·moh·lah·dah_	marmalade
masło _mahs·woh_	butter
miód _myoot_	honey
mleko _mleh·koh_	milk
omlet _ohm·leht_	omelet
parówki _pah·roof·kee_	sausage
płatki śniadaniowe _pwaht·kee shn'yah·dah·n'yoh·veh_	cereal
ser _sehr_	cheese
tost _tohst_	toast
woda _voh·dah_	water

Śniadanie (breakfast) is usually served between 07:00 and 10:00 a.m. **Obiad** (lunch) is the main meal, traditionally enjoyed between 1:00 and 5:00 p.m., but with changing working habits more and more people have their main meal in the evening. **Kolacja** (supper) is typically served from 6:00 p.m. onwards.

Appetizers

grillowany oscypek _gree·loh·vah·nyh ohs·tsyh·pehk_	grilled and smoked ewe's milk cheese
grzybki marynowane _gzhyhp·kee mah·ryh·noh·vah·neh_	marinated wild mushrooms
naleśniki z kapustą i grzybami _nah·lehsh·n'ee·kee skah·poos·tohm ee gzhyh·bah·mee_	thin pancakes with sauerkraut and mushrooms

pieczarki w śmietanie *pyeh-chahr-kee* mushrooms in a cream sauce
fsh'myeh-tah-n'yeh

sałatka *sah-waht-kah* mixed salad

sałatka jarzynowa *sah-waht-kah* mixed vegetable salad in
yah-zhyh-noh-vah mayonnaise

sałatka pomidorowa z cebulą *sah-waht-kah* tomato and onion salad
poh-mee-doh-roh-vah stseh-boo-lohm

sałatka ziemniaczana *sah-waht-kah* potato salad
zh'yehm-n'yah-chah-nah

śledź w oleju *sh'lehdj' voh-leh-yoo* herring in oil

śledź w śmietanie *sh'lehch' fsh'myeh-tah-n'yeh* herring in sour cream

węgorz wędzony *vehn-gohsh vehn-dzoh-nyh* smoked eel

Soup

barszcz czerwony *bahrshch chehr-voh-nyh* beet soup

bulion z pasztecikiem *bool-yohn* consommé with meat-filled
spahsh-teh-ch'ee-kyehm pastries

chłodnik z botwinki *hwohd-n'eek* a cold soup with sour cream,
sboht-feen-kee beets and dill, served with
boiled eggs

grochówka *groh-hoof-kah* pea soup

jarzynowa *yah-zhyh-noh-vah* vegetable soup

kapuśniak *kah-poo-sh'-n'yahk* sauerkraut soup

ogórkowa *oh-goor-koh-vah* pickled cucumber soup

pomidorowa z ryżem/makaronem tomato soup with rice/
poh-mee-doh-roh-vah z ryh-zhehm/ noodles
mah-kah-roh-nehm

rosół (z kury) *roh-soow (skoo-ryh)* (chicken) broth

szczawiowa *shchah-vyoh-vah* sorrel soup with boiled eggs

żurek (z białą kiełbasą) *zhoo-rehk* sour rye soup (with white
(zbyah-whom kyehw-bah-sohm) sausage)

Fish & Seafood

dorsz *dohrsh*	cod
flądra *flohn·drah*	flounder [plaice]
homar *hoh·mahr*	lobster
karp *kahrp*	carp
karp po żydowsku *kahrp poh zhyh·doh·skoo*	carp Jewish style: seasoned and cooked in beer
karp smażony *kahrp smah·zhoh·nyh*	fried carp
krewetki *kreh·veht·kee*	shrimp [prawns]
leszcz *lehshch*	bream
łosoś *woh·sohsh'*	salmon
łupacz *woo·pahch'*	haddock
makrela *mahk·reh·lah*	mackerel
owoce morza *oh·voh·tseh moh·zhah*	seafood
pstrąg *pstrohnk*	trout
rak *rahk*	crayfish
ryba *ryh·bah*	fish
sandacz *sahn·dahch*	perch
sandacz po polsku *sahn·dahch poh pohls·koo*	perch in vegetable stock served with boiled eggs
śledź *sh'lehch'*	herring
szczupak (faszerowany) *shchoo·pahk (fah·sheh·roh·vah·nyh)*	(stuffed) pike
tuńczyk *toon'·chyhk*	tuna
węgorz *vehn·gohsh*	eel

Meat & Poultry

baranina *bah·rah·n'eeh·nah*	mutton
bigos *bee·gohs*	sauerkraut with meat, prunes and mushrooms
boczek *boh·chehk*	bacon

cielęcina *ch'yeh·lehn'·ch'ee·nah*	veal
drób *droop*	poultry
gęś *gehn'sh'*	goose
gołąbki *goh·wohmp·kee*	cabbage leaves stuffed with ground meat and rice
golonka *goh·lohn·kah*	pork shank
gulasz wieprzowy *goo·lahsh vyehp·shoh·vyh*	chopped pork with onions, pepper, garlic and tomato purée
indyk *een·dyhk*	turkey
jagnię *yahg·n'yeh*	lamb
kaczka *kahch·kah*	duck
kaczka pieczona z jabłkami *kahch·kah pyeh·choh·nah zyahp·kah·mee*	roast duck with apples
kiełbasa *kyehw·bah·sah*	sausage
klopsy *klohp·syh*	meatballs
kluski śląskie *kloos·kee sh'lohns·kyeh*	Silesian dumplings
kotlety schabowe *koht·leh·tyh s·hah·boh·veh*	breaded pork chops
kurczak *koor·chahk*	chicken
mięso *myehn·soh*	meat
ozór *oh·zoor*	tongue
pierogi z... *pyeh·roh·gee z...*	dumplings stuffed with...
mięsem *myehn·sehm*	meat
schab pieczony ze śliwkami *s·hahp pyeh·choh·nyh zeh sh'leef·kah·mee*	roast pork loin with prunes
stek *stehk*	steak
szynka *shyhn·kah*	ham
wieprzowina *vyehp·shoh·vee·nah*	pork
wołowina *voh·woh·vee·nah*	beef
zrazy *zrah·zyh*	rolled beef fillets

Vegetables & Staples

bakłażan *bahk•wah•zhahn*	eggplant [aubergine]
brokuł *broh•koow*	broccoli
brukselka *brook•sehl•kah*	Brussel sprout
burak *boo•rahk*	beet
cebula *tseh•boo•lah*	onion
cukinia *tsoo•kee•n'yah*	zucchini [courgette]
czosnek *chohs•nehk*	garlic
fasolka szparagowa *fah•sohl•kah shpah•rah•goh•vah*	green bean
groszek *groh•shehk*	pea
jarzyna *yah•zhyh•nah*	vegetable
kalafior *kah•lah•fyohr*	cauliflower
kapusta *kah•poos•tah*	cabbage
knedle ze śliwkami *knehd•leh zeh sh'leef•kah•mee*	dumplings stuffed with plums
leniwe pierogi *leh•n'ee•veh pyeh•roh•gee*	large dumplings made with flour, potatoes and curd cheese
marchew *mahr•hehf*	carrot
mieszane jarzyny *myeh•shah•neh yah•zhyh•nyh*	mixed vegetables

ogórek *oh-goo-rehk*	cucumber
papryka *pahp-ryh-kah*	pepper
pieczarka/grzyb *pyeh-chahr-kah/gzhyhb*	mushroom/wild mushroom
pierogi z... *pyeh-roh-gee z...*	dumplings stuffed with...
grzybami *gzhyh-bah-mee*	mushrooms
kapustą *kah-poos-tohm*	sauerkraut
serem *seh-rehm*	curd cheese
owocami *oh-voh-tsah-mee*	fruit
pierogi ruskie *pyeh-roh-gee roos-kyeh*	potato and curd cheese dumplings
placki ziemniaczane *plahts-kee zyehm-n'yah-chah-neh*	potato pancakes
pomidor *poh-mee-dohr*	tomato
rzepa *zheh-pah*	turnip
sałata *sah-wah-tah*	lettuce
seler naciowy *seh-lehr nah-ch'yoh-vyh*	celery
ziemniak *z'yehm-n'yahk*	potato
chleb *hlehp*	bread
ryż *ryhsh*	rice
mąka (pszenna) *mohn-kah (pshehn-nah)*	(wheat) flour
makaron *mah-kah-rohn*	pasta
cukier *tsoo-kyehr*	sugar

Fruit

agrest *ahg-rehst*	gooseberry
ananas *ah-nah-nahs*	pineapple
arbuz *ahr-boos*	watermelon
banan *bah-nahn*	banana
brzoskwinia *bzhohs-kfee-n'yah*	peach
cytryna *tsyh-tryh-nah*	lemon
czereśnia *cheh-resh'-n'yah*	cherry

grejpfrut _grehyp_·froot	grapefruit
jabłko _yahp_·koh	apple
limonka lee·_mohn_·kah	lime
malina mah·_lee_·nah	raspberry
morela mo·_reh_·lah	apricot
owoce oh·_voh_·tseh	fruit
pomarańcza poh·mah·_rahn'_·chah	orange
porzeczka czarna/czerwona poh·_zhech_·kah _chahr_·nah/chehr·_voh_·nah	black/red currant
śliwka _sh'leef_·kah	plum
truskawka troos·_kahf_·kah	strawberry
winogrono vee·noh·_groh_·noh	grape

Cheese

biały ser _byah_·wyh sehr	cottage cheese
bryndza _bryhn_·dzah	ewe's milk cheese
camembert kah·_mehm_·behr	camembert
ser sehr	cheese
ser pleśniowy sehr plehsh'·_n'yoh_·vyh	blue cheese
ser topiony _seh_·ryh tohp·_yoh_·nyh	processed cheese
ser żółty _seh_·ryh _zhoow_·tyh	hard cheese
twarożek tfah·_roh_·zhehk	curd cheese

Dessert

deser _deh_·sehr	dessert
galaretka z bitą śmietaną gah·lah·_reht_·kah _zbee_·tohm sh'myeh·_tah_·nohm	fruit jelly with whipped cream
gruszki w syropie _groosh_·kee fsyh·_roh_·pyeh	pears in syrup
kompot owocowy _kohm_·poht oh·voh·_tsoh_·vyh	fruit compote
lody… _loh_·dyh…	…ice cream
czekoladowe cheh·koh·lah·_doh_·veh	chocolate
malinowe mah·lee·_noh_·veh	raspberry

pistacjowe *pees·tats·yoh·veh*	pistachio
śmietankowe *sh'myeh·tahn·koh·veh·*	cream flavored
truskawkowe *troos·kahf·koh·veh*	strawberry
waniliowe *vah·n'eel·yoh·veh*	vanilla
murzynek *moo·zhyh·nek*	chocolate cake with chocolate icing
naleśniki *nah·lesh'·n'ee·kee*	thin pancakes
owoce z bitą śmietaną *oh·voh·tseh zbee·tohm sh'myeh·tah·nohm*	fruit with whipped cream
racuchy z jabłkami *rah·tsoo·hyh z yahp·kah·mee*	small fried pancakes made with sliced apples
sernik *sehr·n'eek*	cheesecake
szarlotka *shahr·loht·kah*	apple tart

Sauces & Condiments

keczup *keh·choop*	ketchup
majonez *mah·yoh·nehs*	mayonaise
musztarda *moosh·tahr·dah*	mustard
oliwa *oh·lee·vah*	oil
pieprz *pyehpsh*	pepper
sól *sool*	salt
ocet *oh·tseht*	vinegar

At the Market

Where are the carts [trolleys]/baskets?	**Gdzie są wózki/koszyki?** *gdj'yeh sohm voos·kee/koh·shyh·kee*
Where is/are…?	**Gdzie jest/są…?** *gdj'yeh yehst/sohm…*
I'd like some of that/this…	**Poproszę trochę tego/tamtego…** *poh·proh·sheh troh·heh teh·goh/tahm·teh·goh…*
Can I taste it?	**Mogę spróbować?** *moh·geh sproo·boh·vahch'*
More/Less.	**Trochę więcej/mniej.** *troh·heh vyehn·tsehy/mn'yehy*
How much?	**Ile to kosztuje?** *ee·leh toh kohsh·too·yeh*

I'd like...	**Poproszę...** *poh•proh•sheh...*
a kilo/half-kilo of...	**kilo/pół kilo...** *kee•loh/poow kee•loh...*
a liter/half-liter of...	**litr/pół litra...** *leetr/poow leet•rah...*
a piece of...	**kawałek...** *kah•vah•wehk...*
a slice of...	**plasterek...** *plahs•teh•rehk...*
Where do I pay?	**Gdzie się płaci?** *gdj'yeh sh'yeh pwah•ch'ee*
A bag, please.	**Poproszę torbę.** *poh•proh•sheh tohr•beh*
I'm being helped.	**Już jestem obsługiwany** *m /*
	obsługiwana *f. joosh yehs•tehm*
	ohp•swoo•gee•vah•nyh/ohp•swoo•gee•vah•nah

For Conversion Tables, see page 176.

YOU MAY HEAR...

Czym mogę służyć? *chyhm moh•geh* *swoo•zhyhch'*	Can I help you?
Co dla pana? *tsoh dlah pah•nah*	What would you like?
Coś jeszcze? *tsohsh' yehsh•cheh*	Anything else?
To wszystko? *toh fshyhs•tkoh*	Is that all?
(To będzie)...złotych. *(toh behn•dj'yeh)...* *zwoh•tyhh*	(That's)...zlotys.

Measurements in Europe are metric – and that applies to the weight of food too. If you tend to think in pounds and ounces, it's worth brushing up on what the metric equivalent is before you go shopping for fruit and veg in markets and supermarkets. Five hundred grams, or half a kilo, is a common quantity to order, and that converts to just over a pound (17.65 ounces, to be precise).

YOU MAY SEE…

NAJLEPIEJ SPOŻYĆ PRZED…	best if used by…
KALORIE	calories
BEZ TŁUSZCZU	fat free
PRZECHOWYWAĆ W LODÓWCE	keep refrigerated
MOŻE ZAWIERAĆ ŚLADOWE ILOŚCI…	may contain traces of…
SPRZEDAĆ PRZED	sell by

In the Kitchen

bottle opener	**otwieracz do butelek** *oht-fyeh-rahch doh boo-teh-lehk*
bowl	**miska** *mees-kah*
can opener	**otwieracz do puszek** *oht-fyeh-rahch doh poo-shehk*
corkscrew	**korkociąg** *kohr-koh-ch'yohnk*
cup	**filiżanka** *fee-lee-zhahn-kah*
fork	**widelec** *vee-deh-lehts*
frying pan	**patelnia** *pah-tehl-n'yah*
glass (non-alcoholic/ alcoholic)	**szklanka/kieliszek** *shklahn-kah/kyeh-lee-shehk*
knife	**nóż** *noosh*
measuring cup/spoon	**miarka kuchenna/łyżka do odmierzania** *myahr-kah koo-hehn-nah/wyhsh-kah doh ohd-myeh-zhah-n'yah*
napkin	**serwetka** *sehr-veht-kah*
plate	**talerz** *tah-lehsh*
pot	**garnek** *gahr-nehk*
saucepan	**rondel** *rohn-dehl*
spatula	**łopatka** *woh-paht-kah*
spoon	**łyżka** *wyhsh-kah*
teaspoon	**łyżeczka** *wyh-zhehch'-kah*

Drinks

ESSENTIAL

Can I see the wine list/ drink menu?	**Czy mogę prosić kartę win/listę drinków?** *chyh moh·geh proh·sheech' kahr·teh veen/lees·teh dreen·koof*
What do you recommend?	**Co może pan polecić?** *tsoh moh·zheh pahn poh·leh·ch'eech'*
I'd like a bottle/glass of red/white wine.	**Poproszę butelkę/kieliszek czerwonego/białego wina.** *poh·proh·sheh boo·tehl·keh/kyeh·lee·shehk chehr·voh·neh·goh/byah·weh·goh vee·nah*
The house wine, please.	**Poproszę wino stołowe.** *poh·proh·sheh vee·noh stoh·woh·veh*
Another bottle/glass, please.	**Poproszę jeszcze jedną butelkę/jeden kieliszek.** *poh·proh·sheh yehsh·cheh jehd·nohm boo·tehl·keh/yeh·dehn kyeh·lee·shehk*
I'd like a local beer.	**Poproszę lokalne piwo.** *poh·proh·sheh loh·kahl·neh pee·voh*

Can I buy you a drink?	**Mogę postawić panu drinka?** _moh_•geh _pohs_•_tah_•veech' _pah_•noo _dreen_•kah
Cheers!	**Na zdrowie!** nah _zdroh_•vyeh
A coffee/tea, please.	**Poproszę kawę/herbatę.** poh•_proh_•sheh _kah_•veh/ hehr•_bah_•teh
Black	**Czarną** _chahr_•nohm
A coffee with..., please.	**Poproszę kawę z...** poh•_proh_•sheh _kah_•veh z...
milk	**mlekiem** _mleh_•kyehm
sugar	**cukrem** _tsook_•rehm
artificial sweetener	**słodzikiem** swoh•_dj'ee_•kyehm
I'd like...	**Poproszę...** poh•_proh_•sheh...
a juice	**sok** sohk
a cola	**colę** _koh_•leh
a (sparkling/still) water	**wodę (gazowaną/niegazowaną)** _voh_•deh (gah•zoh•_vah_•nohm/n'yeh•gah•zoh•_vah_•nohm)
Is the tap water safe to drink?	**Można pić wodę z kranu?** _mohzh_•nah peech' _voh_•deh _skrah_•noo

Non-alcoholic Drinks

cola _koh_•lah	cola
gorąca czekolada goh•_rohn_•tsah cheh•koh•_lah_•dah	hot chocolate
herbata... hehr•_bah_•tah...	tea...
czarna _chahr_•nah	black
owocowa oh•voh•_tsoh_•vah	fruit
zielona zh'yeh•_loh_•nah	green
ziołowa zh'yoh•_woh_•vah	herbal
z cukrem _stsook_•rehm	with sugar
z cytryną stsyht•_ryh_•nohm	with lemon

kawa... _kah•vah..._	coffee...
z mlekiem _zmleh•kyehm_	with milk
z cukrem _stsook•rehm_	with sugar
czarna _chahr•nah_	black
bezkofeinowa _behs•koh•feh•ee•noh•vah_	decaffeinated
z ekspresu _zehks•preh•soo_	espresso
po turecku _poh too•rehts•koo_	Turkish
lemoniada _leh•moh•n'yah•dah_	lemonade
mleko _mleh•koh_	milk
shake _shehyk_	milk shake
sok... _sohk..._	...juice
grejpfrutowy _grehyp•froo•toh•vyh_	grapefruit
pomarańczowy _poh•mah•rahn'•choh•vyh_	orange
jabłkowy _yahp•koh•vyh_	apple
owocowy _sohk oh•voh•tsoh•vyh_	juice
świeżo wyciskany _sh'fyeh•zho_ _vyh•ch'ees•kah•nyh_	fresh squeezed
woda gazowana/niegazowana _voh•dah_ _gah•zoh•vah•nah/n'yeh•gah•zoh•vah•nah_	sparkling/still water

---

Tea is a popular beverage in Poland, usually enjoyed black or
with lemon. Traditionally, **esencja** (the essence) was brewed in
a small ceramic teapot over a boiling kettle. The essence was poured
into a glass or cup and boiling water was added. Nowadays, tea bags
are frequently used. Other types of tea, such as green, fruit or herbal
tea, have become increasingly popular. Coffee is also popular, and
many drink instant coffee at home. Specialty coffee, including espresso
and mocha, is available at many of the numerous **kawiarnie** (coffee
shops) in town.

YOU MAY HEAR...

Czy mogę postawić panu coś do picia? *chyh moh·geh pohs·tah·vich' pah·noo tsosh' doh pee·ch'yah* — Can I get you a drink?

Z mlekiem i z cukrem? *z mleh·kyehm ee stsook·rehm* — With milk and sugar?

Gazowana czy niegazowana? *gah·zoh·vah·nah chyh n'yeh gah·zoh·vah·nah* — Sparkling or still water?

Aperitifs, Cocktails & Liqueurs

ajerkoniak *ah·yehr·koh·n'yahk*	egg-yolk liqueur
gin *djeen*	gin
koniak *koh·n'yahk*	imported brandy
miód pitny *myoot peet·nyh*	mead
szarlotka *shahr·loht·kah*	grass-flavored vodka and apple juice
śliwowica *sh'lee·voh·vee·tsah*	plum brandy
whisky *wees·kee*	whisky
winiak *vee·n'yahk*	Polish brandy
wódka... *voot·kah...*	vodka...
czysta *chyhs·tah*	straight [neat]
z lodem *z loh·dehm*	on the rocks [with ice]
z wodą/tonikiem *z voh·dohm/ toh·n'ee·kyehm*	with water/tonic water
żubrówka *zhoob·roof·kah*	vodka flavored with bison grass

Vodka is one of the best known Polish exports. Several brands, such as Chopin® and Sobieski®, are very popular in the U.S. and U.K. However, the greatest Polish specialty is Żubrówka®, vodka flavored with a unique grass growing only in **Puszcza Białowieska** (Białowieża Forest) in eastern Poland. The grass lends Bison Vodka its unmistakeable taste and characteristic yellowish color. Vodka is served cold and enjoyed from small glasses or mixed with juice or soda. Flavored vodka is also popular.

Vodka, made from either potatoes or rye, is still the national drink, but beer has recently become equally popular.

Polish beer includes Żywiec™, Tyskie™, Lech™ and Warka™; most well-known international brands can also be found.

Beer

piwo... _pee·voh..._		beer...
bezalkoholowe _behz·ahl·koh·hoh·loh·veh_		non-alcoholic
butelkowe/beczkowe _boo·tehl·koh·veh/ behch·koh·veh_		bottled/draft [draught]
ciemne/jasne _ch'yehm·neh/yahs·neh_		dark/light
jasne pełne _yahs·neh pehw·neh_		lager
lokalne _loh·kahl·neh_		local
pilsner _peel·znehr_		pilsner

Wine

wino... _vee·noh..._		...wine
białe _byah·weh_		white
czerwone _chehr·voh·neh_		red
deserowe _deh·seh·roh·veh_		dessert
musujące _moo·soo·yohn·tseh_		sparkling

On the Menu

ajerkoniak *ah·yehr·koh·n'yahk*
liqueur made from egg yolks, aromatic spirits, sugar, vanilla and brandy

agrest *ahg·rehst*
gooseberry

alkohol *ahl·koh·hohl*
alcohol

ananas *ah·nah·nahs*
pineapple

arbuz *ahr·boos*
watermelon

awokado *ah·voh·kah·doh*
avocado

babeczka *bah·behch·kah*
scone

bakłażan *bahk·wah·zhahn*
eggplant [aubergine]

banan *bah·nahn*
banana

baranina *bah·rah·n'ee·nah*
mutton

baranina pieczona ze śmietaną *bah·rah·n'ee·nah pyeh·choh·nah zeh sh'myeh·tah·nohm*
roast mutton with sour cream

barszcz (czerwony) *bahrshch (chehr·voh·nyh)*
(red) beet [beetroot] soup

bażant *bah·zhahnt*
pheasant

bazylia *bah·zyhl·yah*
basil

befsztyk tatarski *behf·shtyhk tah·tahrs·kee*
steak tartare

beza *beh·zah*
meringue

bezkofeinowa *behs·koh·feh·ee·noh·vah*	decaffeinated
biała kapusta *byah·wah kah·poos·tah*	white cabbage
białko *byahw·koh*	egg white
biały ser *byah·wyh sehr*	cottage cheese
bigos *bee·gohs*	sauerkraut with slices of meat, pork sausage, prunes and mushrooms
biszkopt *beesh·kohpt*	sponge cake
bita śmietana *bee·tah sh'myeh·tah·nah*	whipped cream
boczek *boh·chehk*	bacon
brokuł *broh·koow*	broccoli
brukiew *broo·kyehf*	rutabaga [swede]
brukselka *brook·sehl·kah*	Brussels sprout
bryndza *bryhn·dzah*	ewe's milk cheese
brzoskwinia *bzhohs·kfee·n'yah*	peach
budyń *boo·dyhn'*	pudding
budyń z karmelem *boo·dyhn' skahr·meh·lehm*	caramel pudding
bulion *boo·lyohn*	clear soup
bułka *boow·kah*	roll
bułka tarta *boow·kah tahr·tah*	bread crumbs
burak *boo·rahk*	beet [beetroot]
cebula *tseh·boo·lah*	onion
chipsy *cheep·syh*	chips [crisps]
chleb *hlehp*	bread
chleb pszenny *hlehp pshehn·nyh*	wheat bread
chleb razowy *hlehp rah·zoh·vyh*	whole-wheat [wholemeal] bread
chleb żytni *hlehp zhyht·nee*	rye bread
chłodnik *hwohd·n'eek*	cold yogurt, dill and beet [beetroot] soup
chrupki *hroop·kee*	corn snacks

chrzan *hshahn* — horseradish
ciasteczko *ch'yahs•tehch•koh* — cookie [biscuit]
ciasto *ch'yahs•toh* — pastry, cake
ciasto francuskie *ch'yahs•toh frahn•tsoos•kyeh* — puff pastry
ciasto z bakaliami *ch'yahs•toh zbah•kah•yah•mee* — dried fruit cake
ciecierzyca *ch'yeh•ch'yeh•zhyh•tsah* — chick pea
cielęcina *ch'yeh•lehn'•ch'ee•nah* — veal
comber *cohm•behr* — loin (usually game)
cukier *tsoo•kyehr* — sugar
cukinia *tsoo•kee•n'yah* — zucchini [courgette]
ćwikła *ch'feek•wah* — horseradish with beets [beetroot]

cykoria *tsyh•koh•ryah* — endive
cynamon *tsyh•nah•mohn* — cinnamon
cytryna *tsyh•tryh•nah* — lemon
czarna *chahr•nah* — black (coffee)
czarna porzeczka *chahr•nah poh•zhehch•kah* — black currant
czarny chleb *czahr•nyh hlehp* — dark bread
czekolada *cheh•koh•lah•dah* — chocolate
czereśnia *cheh•rehsh•n'yah* — cherry
czerwona fasola *chehr•voh•nah fah•soh•lah* — kidney bean
czerwona kapusta *chehr•voh•nah kah•poos•tah* — red cabbage
czerwone *chehr•voh•neh* — red (wine)
czerwony pieprz *cher•voh•nyh pyehpsh* — chilli pepper
czosnek *chohs•nehk* — garlic
daktyl *dahk•tyhl* — date
deser *deh•sehr* — dessert
domowy *doh•moh•vyh* — homemade
dorsz *dohrsh* — cod
drink *dreenk* — alcoholic drink

drób *droop*	poultry
dymka *dyhm·kah*	spring onion
dynia *dyh·n'yah*	pumpkin
dżem *djehm*	jam
dziczyzna *dj'ee·chyhz·nah*	game
dzik *dj'eek*	wild boar
estragon *ehs·trah·gohn*	tarragon
fasola *fah·soh·lah*	bean
fasolka szparagowa *fah·sohl·kah shpah·rah·goh·vah*	green bean
figa suszona/świeża *fee·gah soo·shoh·nah/ sh'vyeh·zhah*	dried/fresh fig
flądra *flohn·drah*	flounder [plaice]
flaki *flah·kee*	tripe
frytki *fryht·kee*	French fries [chips]
galaretka *gah·lah·reht·kah*	jelly
gałka muszkatołowa *gaw·kah moosh·kah·toh·woh·vah*	nutmeg
gęś *gehn'sh'*	goose
gęsty *gehns·tyh*	rich (sauce)
gin z tonikiem *djeen stoh·nee·kyehm*	gin and tonic
głowizna *gwoh·veez·nah*	pig's head [brawn]
gołąbki *goh·whomp·kee*	ground [minced] meat with rice rolled in cabbage leaves
golonka *goh·lohn·kah*	pork shank
gorąca czekolada *goh·rohn·tsah cheh·koh·lah·dah*	hot chocolate
gorzki *gohsh·kee*	bitter
goździki *gozh'·dj'ee·kee*	cloves
grejpfrut *greyp·froot*	grapefruit
grochówka *groh·hoof·kah*	pea soup

groszek *groh·shehk*	pea
groszek cukrowy *groh·shehk tsook·roh·vyh*	sugarsnap pea
gruszka *groosh·kah*	pear
gruszki w syropie *groosh·kee fsyh·roh·pyeh*	pears in syrup
grzane wino *gzhah·neh vee·noh*	mulled wine
grzyb *gzhyhb*	wild mushroom
gulasz *goo·lahsh*	meat stewed in gravy
gulasz wieprzowy *goo·lahsh vyep·shoh·vyh*	pork stew
gulasz z jagnięcia *goo·lahsh zyahg·nyehn'·ch'yah*	lamb stew
herbata *hehr·bah·tah*	tea
herbatnik *hehr·baht·n'eek*	biscuit
homar *hoh·mahr*	lobster
imbir *eem·beer*	ginger
indyk *een·dyhk*	turkey
jabłko *yahp·koh*	apple
jagnię *yahg·n'yeh*	lamb
jagoda *yah·goh·dah*	blueberry
jajecznica *yah·yehch·n'ee·tsah*	scrambled eggs
jajko *yahy·koh*	egg
jajko na miękko *yahy·koh nah myenk·koh*	soft-boiled egg
jajko na twardo *yahy·koh nah tfahr·doh*	hard-boiled egg
jajko sadzone *yahy·koh sah·dzoh·neh*	fried egg
jarzyna *yah·zhyh·nah*	vegetable
jeżyna *yeh·zhyh·nah*	blackberry
jogurt *yoh·goort*	yogurt
kabaczek *kah·bah·chehk*	marrow
kaczka *kahch·kah*	duck
kaczka pieczona z jabłkami *kahch·kah pyeh·choh·nah z yahp·kah·mee*	roast duck with apples
kalafior *kah·lah·fyohr*	cauliflower

kałamarnica *kah·wah·mahr·n'ee·tsah*   squid

kanapka *kah·nahp·kah*   sandwich

kapary *kah·pah·ryh*   capers

kapuśniak *kah·poosh'·n'yahk*   sauerkraut soup

kapusta *kah·poos·tah*   cabbage

kapusta kiszona *kah·poos·tah kee·shoh·nah*   sauerkraut

karczoch *kahr·chohh*   artichoke

karp *kahrp*   carp

karp po żydowsku *kahrp poh zhyh·dohs·koo*   carp with spices cooked in beer

karp smażony *kahrp smah·zhoh·nyh*   fried carp

kaszanka *kah·shahn·kah*   black pudding

kasztan *kahsh·tah·nyh*   chestnut (sweet)

kawa *kah·vah*   coffee

kawa rozpuszczalna *kah·vah rohs·poosh·chahl·nah*   instant coffee

kawior *kah·vyohr*   caviar

kefir *keh·feer*   thin yogurt

kiełbasa *kyehw·bah·sah*   sausage

kiełbaska wieprzowa *kyehw·bahs·kah vyehp·shoh·vah*   pork sausage

kiełek fasoli *kyeh·wehk fah·soh·lee*   bean sprout

kisiel _kee·sh'ehl_	jelly
kiwi _kee·vee_	kiwi
klops _klohps_	meatball
kluski _kloos·kee_	noodles, dumplings
kluski śląskie _kloos·kee sh'lohns·kyeh_	Silesian dumplings
kminek _kmee·nehk_	caraway
knedle ze śliwkami _knehd·leh zeh shleef·kah·mee_	dumplings stuffed with plums
kokos _koh·kohs_	coconut
kompot _kohm·poht_	stewed fruit
koper _koh·pehr_	fennel
koperek _koh·peh·rehk_	dill
kopytka _koh·pyht·kah_	small potato dumplings
korniszon _kohr·n'ee·shohn_	gherkin
kość _kohsh'ch'_	bone
kotlet _koht·leht_	chop
kotlet schabowy _koht·leht s·hah·boh·vyh_	pork chop fried and breaded
kozie mleko _koh·zh'yeh mleh·koh_	goat's milk
krab _krahp_	crab
krakers _krah·kehrs_	cracker
krewetka _kreh·veht·kah_	shrimp [prawn]
krokiet _kroh·kyeht_	croquette
królik _kroo·leek_	rabbit
krupnik _kroop·neek_	barley soup
kukurydza _koo·koo·ryh·dzah_	corn
kurczak _koor·chahk_	chicken
kurczak grillowany _koor·chahk gree·loh·vah·nyh_	grilled chicken
kurczak pieczony _koor·chahk pyeh·choh·nyh_	roast chicken
kurczak smażony _koor·chahk smah·zhoh·nyh_	fried chicken
kurka _koor·kah_	chanterelle mushroom

kuropatwa *koo·roh·paht·fah*	partridge
kwaśny *kfahsh'·nyh*	sour (taste)
łagodny *wah·gohd·neh*	mild (flavor)
langusta *lahn·goos·tah*	lobster
lekki *lehk·kee*	light (sauce)
lemoniada *leh·moh·n'yah·dah*	lemonade
leniwe pierogi *leh·n'ee·veh pyeh·roh·gee*	flour, potato and curd cheese dumplings
leszcz *lehshch*	bream
likier *lee·kyehr*	liqueur
limonka *lee·mohn·kah*	lime
liść laurowy *leesh'ch' lahw·roh·vyh*	bay leaf
lód *loot*	ice
lody *loh·dyh*	ice cream
łopatka *woh·paht·kah*	shoulder (cut of meat)
łosoś *woh·sohsh'*	salmon
łosoś wędzony *woh·sohsh' vehn·dzoh·nyh*	smoked salmon
lukier *loo·kyehr*	icing
łupacz *woo·pahch*	haddock
majonez *mah·yoh·nehs*	mayonnaise
majonez czosnkowy *mah·yoh·nehs chohsn·koh·vyh*	garlic mayonnaise
mąka *mohn·kah*	flour
mąka pszenna *mohn·kah pshehn·nah*	wheat flour
mąka razowa *mohn·kah rah·zoh·vah*	whole-wheat [wholemeal] flour
makaron *mah·kah·rohn*	pasta
makrela *mahk·reh·lah*	mackerel
malina *mah·lee·nah*	raspberry
małża *mahw·zhah*	mussel
mandarynka *mahn·dah·ryhn·kah*	tangerine

marcepan *mahr·tseh·pahn*	marzipan
marchew *mahr·hehf*	carrot
margaryna *mahr·gah·ryh·nah*	margarine
marmolada *mahr·moh·lah·dah*	marmalade
marynowany w occie *mah·ryh·noh·vah·nyh vohts·ch'yeh*	marinated in vinegar
maślanka *mahsh'·lahn·kah*	buttermilk
masło *mahs·woh*	butter
mazurek *mah·zoo·rehk*	Easter shortcake (various flavors)
melasa *meh·lah·sah*	molasses [treacle]
melon *meh·lohn*	melon
miecznik *myehch·n'eek*	swordfish
mielona wołowina *myeh·loh·nah voh·woh·vee·nah*	minced beef
mięso *myehn·soh*	meat
mięso grillowane *myehn·soh gree·loh·vah·neh*	grilled meat
mieszane jarzyny *myeh·shah·neh yah·zhyh·nyh*	mixed vegetables
mięta *myehn·tah*	mint
migdał *meeg·dahw*	almond
migdały w cukrze *meeg·dah·wyh ftsook·sheh*	sugared almonds
miód *myoot*	honey
miód pitny *myoot peet·nyh*	mead
mizeria *mee·zeh·ryah*	cucumber salad with sour cream
mleko *mle·koh*	milk
młoda kapusta *mwoh·dah kah·poos·tah*	spring cabbage
młody kurczak *mwoh·dyh koor·chahk*	spring chicken
mocne *mohts·neh*	full-bodied (wine), strong (beer)

morela *moh·reh·lah*	apricot
morwa *mohr·vah*	mulberry
mrożony *mroh·zhoh·nyh*	iced (drinks)
mus *moos*	mousse
musujący *moo·soo·yohn·tsyh*	sparkling
musztarda *moosh·tahr·dah*	mustard
naleśnik *nah·lehsh'·n'eek*	thin pancake
naleśniki z kapustą i grzybami *nah·lehsh'·n'ee·kee skah·poos·tohm ee gzhyh·bah·mee*	thin pancakes with sauerkraut and mushrooms
napój *nah·puy*	soft drink
nektarynka *nehk·tah·ryhn·kah*	nectarine
nerka *nehr·kah*	kidney
nerkówka *nehr·koof·kah*	loin (cut of meat)
noga *noh·gah*	leg (cut of meat)
nóżki *noosh·kee*	pigs' feet
nugat *noo·gaht*	nougat
ogon *oh·gohn*	oxtail
ogórek *oh·goo·rehk*	cucumber
ogórek kiszony *oh·goo·rehk kee·shoh·nyh*	dill pickle
ogórek konserwowy *oh·goo·rehk kohn·sehr·voh·vyh*	pickle
ogórkowa *oh·goor·koh·vah*	pickled cucumber soup
okoń *oh·kohn'*	bass
oliwka *oh·leef·kah*	olive
oliwki nadziewane *oh·leef·kee nah·dj'yeh·vah·neh*	stuffed olives
omlet *ohm·leht*	omelet
opieniek *oh·pyeh·n'yehk*	oyster mushroom
oranżada *oh·rahn·zhah·dah*	orangeade
orzech *oh·zhehh*	nut

orzech laskowy _oh·zhehh lahs·koh·vyh_	hazelnut
orzech nerkowca _oh·zhehh nehr·kohf·tsah_	cashew
orzech włoski _oh·zhehh vwohs·kee_	walnut
orzechy mieszane _oh·zheh·hyh myeh·shah·neh_	assorted nuts
orzeszek ziemny _oh·zheh·shehk zh'yehm·nyh_	peanut
orzeszki ziemne solone _oh·zhehsh·kee zh'yehm·neh soh·loh·neh_	salted peanuts
ośmiornica _ohsh'·myohr·nee·tsah_	octopus
ostra kiełbaska _ohs·trah kyehw·bahs·kah_	spicy sausage
ostry (smak) _ohs·tryh (smahk)_	hot, spicy (flavor)
ostryga _ohs·tryh·gah_	oyster
owoce _oh·voh·tseh_	fruit
owoce kandyzowane _oh·voh·tseh kahn·dyh·zoh·vah·neh_	candied fruit
owoce morza _oh·voh·tseh moh·zhah_	seafood
owoce z puszki _oh·voh·tseh spoosh·kee_	canned fruit
owsianka _ohf·sh'yahn·kah_	porridge
ozór _oh·zoor_	tongue
pączek _pohn·chehk_	donut [doughnut]
papryka zielona/czerwona _pahp·ryh·kah zh'yeh·loh·nah/chehr·voh·nah_	green/red pepper
parówka _pah·roof·kah_	sausage
pasternak _pah·stehr·nahk_	parsnip
paszteciki _pahsh·teh·ch'ee·kee_	pastries filled with meat, fish or cabbage
pasztet _pahsh·teht_	pâté
pasztet w galarecie _pahsh·teht vgah·lah·reh·ch'yeh_	pâté in aspic
perliczka _pehr·leech·kah_	guinea fowl
pieczarka _pyeh·chahr·kah_	mushroom

pieczarki w śmietanie *pyeh·chahr·kee vsh'myeh·tah·n'yeh* — mushrooms in cream

pieczeń *pyeh·chehn'* — pot roast

pieczona wołowina *pyeh·choh·nah voh·woh·vee·nah* — roast beef

pieprz *pyehpsh* — pepper (condiment)

pieprzny sos *pyehp·shnyh sohs* — hot pepper sauce

piernik *pyehr·n'eek* — ginger cake

pierogi *pyeh·roh·gee* — stuffed dumplings

pierogi ruskie *pyeh·roh·gee roos·kyeh* — dumplings with cheese and onion

pierogi z kapustą i z grzybami *pyeh·roh·gee skah·poos·tohm ee zgzhyh·bah·mee* — dumplings with sauerkraut and mushrooms

pierogi z mięsem *pyeh·roh·gee zmyehn·sehm* — dumplings with meat

pierogi z owocami *pyeh·roh·gee zoh·voh·tsah·mee* — dumplings with fruit

pierogi z serem *pyeh·roh·gee sseh·rehm* — dumplings with curd cheese

pierś *pyehrsh'* — breast

pierś z kurczaka *pyehrsh' skoor·chah·kah* — breast of chicken

pietruszka zielona *pyeht·roosh·kah zh'yeh·loh·nah* — parsley

pikantny *pee·kahnt·nyh* — spicy

piwo *pee·voh* — beer

piwo jasne pełne *pee·voh yahs·neh pehw·neh* — lager

placek *plah·tsehk* — tart, pie

placki ziemniaczane *plahts·kee zh'yehm·n'yah·chah·neh* — potato pancakes

płatki śniadaniowe *pwaht·kee sh'nyah·dah·n'yoh·veh* — cereal

podroby *pohd·roh·byh* — giblets

polędwica *poh·lehnd·vee·tsah* — tenderloin (cut of meat)

pomarańcza *poh•mah•rahn'•chah* — orange
pomidor *poh•mee•dohr* — tomato
pomidorowa z makaronem/ryżem — tomato soup with noodles/
poh•mee•doh•roh•vah z mah•kah•roh•nehm/ rice
ryh•zhehm
poncz *pohnch* — punch
por *pohr* — leek
porcja *pohr•tsyah* — portion
porto *pohr•toh* — port
potrawa *poh•trah•vah* — dish
potrawka *poh•trahf•kah* — casserole
prosiak *proh•sh'yahk* — suckling pig
przekąski *psheh•kohns•kee* — snacks
przepiórka *psheh•pyoor•kah* — quail
przyprawy *pshyh•prah•vyh* — seasoning, spices
przysmak regionalny *pshyhs•mahk* — local specialty
reh•gyoh•nahl•nyh

pstrąg *pstrohnk* — trout
purée *pee•reh* — purée
purée z ziemniaków *pee•reh* — potato purée
zzh'yehm•n'yah•koof
pyzy *pyh•zyh* — large potato dumplings, sometimes with meat stuffing

rabarbar *rah•bahr•bahr* — rhubarb
racuch *rah•tsooh* — small pancake
racuchy z jabłkami *rah•tsoo•hyh* — apple pancakes, fritters
zyahp•kah•mee
rak *rahk* — crayfish
rodzynki *roh•dzyhn•kee* — raisins
rolmops *rohl•mohps* — pickled herring filet [rollmop herring]

rosół _roh·soow_ — consommé, broth

rosół z kury _roh·soow skoo·ryh_ — chicken broth

rosół z mięsem i jarzynami _roh·soow zmyehn·sehm ee yah·zhyh·nah·mee_ — meat and vegetable broth

rostbef _rohst·behf_ — roast beef

rozmaryn _rohz·mah·ryhn_ — rosemary

rumsztyk _room·shtyhk_ — rumpsteak

ryba _ryh·bah_ — fish

ryż _rysh_ — rice

rzepa _zheh·pah_ — turnip

rzeżucha _zheh·zhoo·hah_ — cress

rzeżucha wodna _zheh·zhoo·hah vohd·nah_ — watercress

rzodkiewka _zhoht·kyehf·kah_ — radish

sałata _sah·wah·tah_ — lettuce

sałatka jarzynowa _sah·waht·kah yah·zhyh·noh·vah_ — mixed vegetable salad

sałatka z kapusty _sah·waht·kah skah·poos·tyh_ — coleslaw

salceson _sahl·tseh·sohn_ — headcheese [brawn]

sandacz _sahn·dahch_ — perch

sandacz po polsku _sahn·dahch poh pohl·skoo_ — perch in vegetable stock with eggs

sardela _sahr·deh·lah_ — anchovy

sardynka _sahr·dyhn·kah_ — sardine

sarnina _sahr·nee·nah_ — venison

schab _s·hahp_ — loin of pork

schab pieczony ze śliwkami _s·hahp pyeh·choh·nyh zeh sh'leef·kah·mee_ — roast pork sirloin with prunes

schłodzony _s·hwoh·dzoh·nyh_ — chilled

seler naciowy _seh·lehr nah·ch'yoh·vyh_ — celery

ser _sehr_ — cheese

ser kozi _sehr koh·zh'ee_ — goat's cheese

ser owczy *sehr ohf•chyh*	ewe's milk cheese
ser pleśniowy *sehr pleh•sh'n'yoh•vyh*	blue cheese
ser topiony *sehr toh•pyoh•nyh*	processed cheese
serce *sehr•tseh*	heart
sernik *sehr•n'eek*	cheesecake
shake *shehyk*	milkshake
śledź *sh'lehch'*	herring
śledź marynowany *sh'lehdj' mah•ryh•noh•vah•nyh*	marinated herring
śledź w oleju *sh'lehdj' voh•leh•yoo*	herring in oil
śledź w śmietanie *sh'lehch' fsh'myeh•tah•n'yeh*	herring in sour cream
ślimak *sh'lee•mahk*	snail
śliwka *sh'leef•kah*	plum
śliwowica *sh'lee•voh•vee•tsah*	plum brandy
słodka papryka *swoht•kah pah•pryh•kah*	sweet red pepper
słodki *swoht•kee*	sweet
słodycze *swoh•dyh•cheh*	candies [sweets]
słodzik *swoh•dj'eek*	sweetener
śmietana *sh'myeh•tah•nah*	cream
soczewica *soh•cheh•vee•tsah*	lentil
sok *sohk*	juice
sok cytrynowy *sohk tsyh•tryh•noh•vyh*	lemon juice
sok owocowy *sohk oh•voh•tsoh•vyh*	fruit juice
sok pomarańczowy *sohk poh•mah•ran'•choh•vyh*	orange juice
sok z limonki *sohk zlee•mohn•kee*	lime juice
sól *sool*	salt
sola *soh•lah*	sole
solony *soh•loh•nyh*	salted
sos *sohs*	sauce
sos czosnkowy *sohs chohsn•koh•vyh*	garlic sauce

sos pomidorowy *sohs poh·mee·doh·roh·vyh*	tomato sauce
sos słodko-kwaśny *sohs swoht·koh·kfahsh'·nyh*	sweet and sour sauce
sos winegret *sohs vee·neh·greh*	vinaigrette [French dressing]
sos z pieczeni *sohs spyeh·cheh·n'ee*	gravy
specjalność szefa kuchni *spehts·yahl·nohsh'ch' sheh·fah kooh·n'ee*	special
stek *stehk*	steak
stek z polędwicy *stehk spoh·lehnd·vee·tsyh*	fillet steak
strucla *stroots·lah*	strudel
suflet *soof·leht*	soufflé
surówka *soo·roof·kah*	fresh vegetable salad
surowy *soo·roh·vyh*	raw
suszone daktyle *soo·shoh·neh dahk·tyh·leh*	dried dates
suszone śliwki *soo·shoh·neh sh'leef·kee*	prunes
świeże owoce *sh'fyeh·zheh oh·voh·tseh*	fresh fruit
świeży *sh'fyeh·zhyh*	fresh
świeży daktyl *sh'fyeh·zhyh dahk·tyhl*	fresh date
syrop *syh·rohp*	syrup
szafran *shahf·rahn*	saffron
szalotka *shah·loht·kah*	shallot
szałwia *shahw·vyah*	sage

szarlotka *shahr·loht·kah*	apple pie; grass-flavored vodka with apple juice
szaszłyk *shahsh·wyhk*	lamb or mutton kebab
szczaw *shchahf*	sorrel
szczawiowa zupa *shchah·vyoh·vah zoo·pah*	sorrel soup
szczupak *shchoo·pahk*	pike
szczupak nadziewany *shchoo·pahk nah·dj'yeh·vah·nyh*	stuffed pike
szczupak w galarecie *shchoo·pahk vgah·lah·reh·ch'yeh*	pike in aspic
szczypiorek *shchyh·pyoh·rehk*	chives
szklanka *shklahn·kah*	glass
sznycel *shnyh·tsehl*	breaded pork or veal cutlet
szparag *shpah·rahg*	asparagus
szpinak *shpee·nahk*	spinach
szprotka *shproht·kah*	sprat (small herring)
sztuka mięsa *shtoo·kah myehn·sah*	portion of meat
szynka *shyhn·kah*	ham
tłusty *twoos·tyh*	fatty
tonik *toh·neek*	tonic water
tort *tohrt*	rich cake
tost *tohst*	toast
trufla *troof·lah*	truffle
truskawka *trus·kahf·kah*	strawberry
tuńczyk *toon'·chyhk*	tuna
twarożek *tfah·roh·zhehk*	fresh curd cheese
tymianek *tyh·myah·nehk*	thyme
udko *oot·koh*	leg (cut of meat)
w cieście *fch'yehsh'·ch'yeh*	in batter
w czosnku *fchohsn·koo*	in garlic
w oliwie *voh·lee·vyeh*	in olive oil

wafel _vah_-felh	waffle
wanilia vah-_n'eel_-yah	vanilla
wątróbka vohn-_troop_-kah	liver
wątróbka z kurczaka vohn-_troop_-kah skoor-_chah_-kah	chicken liver
wędlina vehn-_dlee_-nah	cold cuts
węgorz _vehn_-gohsh	eel
węgorz wędzony _vehn_-gohsh vehn-_dzoh_-nyh	smoked eel
wieprzowina vyehp-shoh-_vee_-nah	pork
winiak _vee_-n'yahk	Polish brandy
wino _vee_-noh	wine
wino deserowe _vee_-noh deh-seh-_roh_-veh	dessert wine
wino musujące _vee_-noh moo-soo-_yohn_-tseh	sparkling wine
wino stołowe _vee_-noh stoh-_woh_-veh	table wine
winogrono vee-noh-_groh_-noh	grape
winogrono czerwone vee-noh-_groh_-noh chehr-_voh_-neh	red grape
winogrono zielone vee-noh-_groh_-noh zh'yeh-_loh_-neh	white grape
wiśnia _veesh'_-n'yah	cherry
woda _voh_-dah	water
woda gazowana _voh_-dah gah-zoh-_vah_-nah	sparkling water
woda gorąca _voh_-dah goh-_rohn_-tsah	hot water
woda mineralna _voh_-dah mee-neh-_rahl_-nah	mineral water
woda niegazowana _voh_-dah n'yeh-gah-zoh-_vah_-nah	still water
woda sodowa _voh_-dah soh-_doh_-vah	soda water
woda z lodem _voh_-dah z_loh_-dehm	iced water
wódka _voot_-kah	vodka
wódki _voot_-kee	spirits
wół voow	ox

wołowina *voh·woh·vee·nah*	beef
z cukrem *stsoo·krehm*	with sugar
z cytryną *stsyh·tryh·nohm*	with lemon
z kością *skohsh'·ch'yohm*	on the bone
zając *zah·yohnts*	hare
zakąski *zah·kohns·kee*	appetizers
zapiekany *zah·pyeh·kah·nyh*	gratin
zboże *zboh·zheh*	grain
żeberka *zheh·behr·kah*	spare ribs
zielona fasolka *zh'yeh·loh·nah fah·sohl·kah*	green bean
zielona sałata *zh'yeh·loh·nah suh·wah·tah*	lettuce
zielony pieprz *zh'yeh·loh·nyh pyehpsh*	green pepper
ziemniak *zh'yehm·n'yahk*	potato
ziemniak pieczony *zh'yehm·n'yahk pyeh·choh·nyh*	baked potato
ziemniaki gotowane *zh'yehm·n'yah·kee goh·toh·vah·neh*	boiled potatoes
zioła mieszane *zh'yoh·wah myeh·shah·neh*	mixed herbs
zioło *zh'yoh·woh*	herb
żółtko *zhoow·tkoh*	egg yolk
żółty ser *zhoow·tyh sehr*	hard cheese
Żubrówka *zhoo·broof·kah*	grass-flavoured vodka
zupa *zoo·pah*	soup
zupa jarzynowa *zoo·pah yah·zhyh·noh·vah*	vegetable soup
zupa krem *zoo·pah krehm*	cream soup
zupa na zimno *zoo·pah nah zh'eem·noh*	cold soup
żurek (z białą kiełbasą) *zhoo·rehk (zbyah·wohm kyeh·bah·sohm)*	sour rye soup (with white sausage)

People

Conversation

ESSENTIAL

Hello	**Dzień dobry.**	dj'yehn' <u>dohb</u>•ryh
How are you?	**Jak się pan ma?**	yahk sh'yeh pahn mah
Fine, thanks.	**W porządku, dziękuję.**	fpoh•<u>zhohnt</u>•koo dz'yehn•koo•yeh
Excuse me!	**Przepraszam!**	psheh•<u>prah</u>•shahm
Do you speak English?	**Mówi pan po angielsku?**	<u>moo</u>•vee pahn poh ahn•<u>gyehl</u>•skoo
What's your name?	**Jak się pan nazywa?**	yahk sh'yeh pahn nah•<u>zyh</u>•vah
My name is...	**Nazywam się...**	nah•<u>zyh</u>•vahm sh'yeh...
Pleased to meet you.	**Miło mi pana poznać.**	<u>mee</u>•woh mee <u>pah</u>•nah <u>pohz</u>•nahch'
Where are you from?	**Skąd pan jest?**	skohnt pahn yehst
I'm from the U.S./U.K.	**Jestem z USA/Wielkiej Brytanii.**	<u>yehs</u>•tehm z oo•ehs•<u>ah</u>/<u>vyehl</u>•kyehy bryh•<u>tah</u>•n'ee
What do you do for a living?	**Czym się pan zajmuje?**	chyhm sh'yeh pahn zahy•<u>moo</u>•yeh
I work for...	**Pracuję w...**	prah•<u>tsoo</u>•yeh v...
I'm a student.	**Studiuję.**	stoo•<u>dyoo</u>•yeh
I'm retired.	**Jestem na emeryturze.**	<u>yehs</u>•tehm nah eh•meh•ryh•<u>too</u>•zheh
Do you like...?	**Lubi pan...?**	<u>loo</u>•bee pahn...
Goodbye.	**Do widzenia.**	doh vee•<u>dzeh</u>•n'yah
See you later.	**Do zobaczenia.**	doh zoh•bah•<u>cheh</u>•n'yah

Language Difficulties

Do you speak English?	**Mówi pan po angielsku?**	_moo_·vee pahn po ahn·_gyehls_·koo
Does anyone here speak English?	**Czy ktoś tu zna angielski?**	chyh ktohsh' too znah ahn·_gyehls_·kee
I don't speak much Polish.	**Słabo mówię po polsku.**	_swah_·boh _moo_·vyeh poh _pohls_·koo
Can you speak more slowly?	**Proszę mówić wolniej.**	_proh_·sheh _moo_·veech' _vohl_·n'yehy
Can you repeat that?	**Proszę powtórzyć.**	_proh_·sheh pohf·_too_·zhyhch'
Excuse me? [Pardon?]	**Słucham?**	_swoo_·hahm
What was that?	**Co pan powiedział?**	tsoh pahn poh·_vyeh_·dj'yahw
Can you spell it?	**Może pan to przeliterować?**	_moh_·zheh pahn toh psheh·leeh·teh·_roh_·vahch'
Can you write it down?	**Może pan mi to napisać?**	_moh_·zheh pahn mee toh nah·_pee_·sahch'
Can you translate this into English for me?	**Może pan mi to przetłumaczyć na angielski?**	_moh_·zheh pahn mee toh psheh·twoo·_mah_·chyhch' nah ahn·_gyehl_·skyh
What does this mean?	**Co to znaczy?**	tsoh toh _znah_·chyh
I understand.	**Rozumiem.**	roh·_zoo_·myehm
I don't understand.	**Nie rozumiem.**	n'yeh roh·_zoo_·myehm
Do you understand?	**Rozumie pan?**	roh·_zoo_·myeh pahn

YOU MAY HEAR...

Słabo mówię po angielsku. _swah_·boh _moo_·vyeh poh ahn·_gyehls_·koo

I speak only a little English.

Nie mówię po angielsku. n'yeh _moo_·vyeh poh ahn·_gyehls_·koo

I don't speak English.

Greetings between Polish men and women have changed during recent years. In the past men kissed women's hands as a sign of respect. Today men and women say hello or kiss each other on the cheek if they are good friends. In most situations you usually say **dzień dobry**, good morning or hello. With relatives, friends and children you can simply say **cześć**, hi.

Making Friends

Hello/Hi!	**Dzień dobry./Cześć!** *dj'yehn' dohb•ryh/chehsh'ch'*
Good morning.	**Dzień dobry.** *dj'yehn' dohb•ryh*
Good evening.	**Dobry wieczór.** *dohb•ryh vyeh•choor*
My name is…	**Nazywam się…** *nah•zyh•vahm sh'yeh…*
What's your name?	**Jak się pan nazywa?** *yahk sh'yeh pahn nah•zyh•vah*
I'd like to introduce you to…	**Chciałbym m /Chciałabym f pana przedstawić…** *hch'yahw•byhm/hch'yah•wah•byhm pah•nah psheht•stah•veech'…*
Pleased to meet you.	**Miło mi pana poznać.** *mee•woh mee pah•nah pohz•nahch'*
How are you?	**Jak się pan ma?** *yahk sh'yeh pahn mah*

| Fine, thanks. | **W porządku, dziękuję.** *fpoh-zhohnt-koo dz'yehn-koo-yeh* |
| And you? | **A pan?** *ah pahn* |

Travel Talk

I'm here...	**Jestem tutaj.** *yehs-tehm too-tay*
on business	**służbowo** *swoozh-boh-voh*
on vacation	**na wakacjach** *nah vah-kahts-yahh*
I'm studying.	**Studiuję.** *stood-yoo-yeh*
I'm staying for...	**Będę tu...** *beh-deh too...*
I've been here...	**Jestem tu...** *yehs-tehm too...*
a day	**jeden dzień** *yeh-dehn dj'yehn'*
a week	**tydzień** *tyh-dj'yehn'*
a month	**miesiąc** *myeh-sh'yohnts*
Where are you from?	**Skąd pan jest?** *skohnt pahn yehst*
I'm from...	**Jestem z...** *yehs-tehm z...*

For Numbers, see page 171.

For Dates, see page 174.

Personal

Who are you with?	**Z kim pan tu jest?** *skeem pahn too yehst*
I'm here alone.	**Jestem sam** *m* **/sama** *f yehs-tehm sahm/sah-mah*
I'm with...	**Jestem z...** *yehs-tehm z...*
my husband/wife	**moim mężem/moją żoną** *moh-eem mehn-zhehm/ moh-yohm zhoh-nohm*
my boyfriend/ girlfriend	**moim chłopakiem/moją dziewczyną** *moh-eem hwoh-pah-kyehm/moh-yohm dj'yehf-chyh-nohm*
a friend	**przyjacielem** *m* **/przyjaciółką** *f pshyh-yah-ch'yeh-lehm/pshyh-yah-ch'yoow-kohm*
friends	**przyjaciółmi** *pshyh-yah-ch'yoow-myh*
a colleague	**kolegą** *m* **/koleżanką** *f* **z pracy** *koh-leh-gohm/ koh-leh-zhahn-kohm sprah-tsyh*

colleagues	**kolegami** m **/koleżankami** f **z pracy**
	koh·leh·gah·myh/koh·leh·zhahn·kah·myh sprah·tsyh
When's your birthday?	**Kiedy ma pan urodziny?** *k'yeh·dyh mah pahn*
	oo·roh·dj'ee·nyh
How old are you?	**Ile ma pan lat?** *ee·leh mah pahn laht*
I'm...	**Mam...lat.** *mahm...laht*
Are you married?	**Czy jest pan żonaty** m **/pani mężatką** f**?** *chyh*
	yehst pahn zhoh·nah·tyh/pah·n'ee mehn·zhaht·kohm
I'm...	**Jestem...** *yehs·tehm...*
single/ in a	**wolny** m **/wolna** f **w związku** *vohl·nyh/vohl·nah/*
relationship	*vzvyohn·skoo*
engaged	**zaręczony** m **/zaręczona** f *zah·rehn·choh·nyh/*
	zah·rehn·choh·nah
married	**żonaty** m **/mężatką** f *zhoh·nah·tyh/*
	mehn·zhaht·kohm
divorced	**rozwiedziony** m **/rozwiedziona** f
	rohz·vyeh·dj'yoh·nyh/rohz·vyeh·dj'yoh·nah
separated	**w separacji** *fseh·pah·rah·tsee*
widowed	**wdowcem** m **/wdową** f *vdoh·vtsehm/vdoh·vohm*
Do you have children/	**Ma pan dzieci/wnuki?** *mah pahn dj'yeh·ch'ee/*
grandchildren?	*vnoo·kee*

For Numbers, see page 171.

Work & School

What do you do for a	**Czym się pan zajmuje?** *chyhm sh'yeh pahn*
living?	*zahy·moo·yeh?*
What are you studying?	**Co pan studiuje?** *tsoh pahn stood·yoo·yeh*
I'm studying...	**Studiuję...** *stood·yoo·yeh...*
I work full time/	**Pracuję na pełny etat/część etatu.** *prah·tsoo·yeh*
part time.	*nah pehw·nyh eh·taht/chehn'sh'ch' eh·tah·too*
I'm unemployed	**Nie pracuję** *n'yeh prah·tsoo·yeh*
I work at home	**Pracuję w domu** *prah·tsoo·yeh vdoh·moo*

Who do you work for?	**Gdzie pan pracuje?** *gdj'yeh pahn prah·tsoo·yeh*
I work for...	**Pracuję w...** *prah·tsoo·yeh v...*
Here's my business card	**Oto moja wizytówka** *oh·toh moh·yah vee·zyh·toof·kah*

For Business Travel, see page 143.

Weather

What's the weather forecast?	**Jaka jest prognoza pogody?** *yah·kah yehst prohg·noh·zah poh·goh·dyh*
What beautiful/ terrible weather!	**Jaka piękna/okropna pogoda!** *yah·kah pyehnk·nah/oh·krohp·nah poh·goh·dah*
It's cool/warm.	**Jest chłodno/ciepło.** *yehst hwohd·noh/ch'yehp·wo*
It's hot/cold.	**Jest gorąco/zimno.** *yehst goh·rohn·tsoh/zh'eem·noh*
It's sunny.	**Świeci słońce.** *sh'vyeh·ch'ee swohn'·tseh*
It's rainy/snowy.	**Pada deszcz/śnieg.** *pah·dah dehshch/sh'n'yehk*
It's icy.	**Jest ślisko.** *yehst sh'lees·koh*
Do I need a jacket/ an umbrella?	**Mam wziąć kurtkę/parasol?** *mahm vzyohn'ch' koort·keh/pah·rah·sohl*

For Temperature, see page 177.

Romance

ESSENTIAL

Would you like to go out for a drink/meal?	**Może pójdziemy na drinka/coś zjeść?** *moh·zheh pooy·dj'eh·myh nah dreen·kah/tsohsh' zyehsh'ch'*
What are your plans for tonight/tomorrow?	**Masz jakieś plany na wieczór/jutro?** *mahsh yah·kyehsh' plah·nyh nah vyeh·choor/yoot·roh*
Can I have your number?	**Podasz mi swój numer telefonu?** *poh·dahsh mee sfuy noo·mehr teh·leh·foh·noo*

Can I join you?	**Mogę się dosiąść?** _moh_•geh sh'yeh _doh_•sh'yohn'sh'ch'
Can I buy you a drink?	**Mogę postawić ci drinka?** _moh_•geh pohs•_tah_•veech' ch'ee _dree_•nkah
I like/love you.	**Lubię/Kocham cię.** _loo_•bieh/_koh_•hahm ch'yeh

For Grammar, see page 166.

The Dating Game

Would you like to go out for…?	**Może pójdziemy na…?** _moh_•zheh pooy•_dj'yeh_•myh nah…
coffee	**kawę** _kah_•veh
a drink	**drinka** _dreen_•kah
dinne	**kolację** koh•_lahts_•yeh
What are your plans for…?	**Masz jakieś plany na…?** mahsh _yah_•kyehsh' _plah_•nyh nah…
today	**dzisiaj** _dj'ee_•sh'yahy
tonight	**wieczór** _vyeh_•choor
tomorrow	**jutro** _yoot_•roh
this weekend	**weekend** _wee_•kehnt

Where would you like to go?	**Dokąd chciałbyś** m **/chciałabyś** f **pójść?** _doh-kohnt_ _hch'yahw-byhsh'/hch'yah-wah-bysh' pooysh'ch'_
I'd like to go to...	**Chciałbym** m **/Chciałabym** f _pójść do..._ _hch'yahw-byhm/hch'yah-wah-byhm pooysh'ch' doh..._
Do you like...?	**Lubisz...?** _loo-beesh'...?_
Can I have your number?	**Podasz mi swój numer telefonu?** _poh-dahsh mee sfooy noo-mehr teh-leh-foh-noo_
Can I have your e-mail?	**Podasz mi swój e-mail?** _poh-dahsh mee sooy ee-mehyl_
Are you on Facebook/ Twitter?	**Masz konto na Facebooku/Twitterze?** _mahsh kohn-toh nah fehys-boo-koo/twee-teh-zheh_
Can I join you?	**Mogę się dosiąść?** _moh-geh sh'yeh doh-sh'yohn'sh'ch'_
Is this seat free?	**To miejsce jest wolne?** _toh myehys-tseh yehst vohl-neh_
You look great!	**Świetnie wyglądasz!** _sh'vyeht-n'yeh wyh-glohn-dahsh_
You're very attractive	**Jesteś bardzo atrakcyjny** m **/atrakcyjna** f _yehs-tehsh' bahr-dzoh ah-trahk-tsyhy-nyh/ ah-trahk-tsyhy-nah_
Let's go somewhere quieter.	**Może pójdziemy w jakieś spokojniejsze miejsce?** _moh-zheh puy-dj'yeh-myh vyah-kyehsh' spoh-kohy-n'yehy-sheh myehys-tseh_

For Communications, see page 47.

Accepting & Rejecting

I'd love to.	**Bardzo chętnie.** _bahr-dzoh chehnt-n'yeh_
Where should we meet?	**Gdzie możemy się spotkać?** _gdj'eh moh-zheh-myh sh'yeh spoht-kach'_
I'll meet you at the bar/ your hotel.	**Spotkamy się w barze/twoim hotelu.** _spoht-kah-myh sh'yeh vbah-zheh/tfoh-eem hoh-teh-loo_
I'll come by at...	**Przyjdę o...** _pshyhy-deh oh..._
What's your address?	**Gdzie mieszkasz?** _gdj'yeh myehsh-kahsh_

I'm busy.	**Jestem zajęty** m **/zajęta** f *yehs*-tehm zah-*yehn*-tyh/ *zah*-*yehn*-tah
I'm not interested.	**Nie jestem zainteresowany** m**/zainteresowana** f *n'yeh yehs*-tehm zah-een-teh-reh-soh-*vah*-nyh/ *zah*-een-teh-reh-soh-*vah*-nah
Leave me alone, please!	**Zostaw mnie w spokoju!** *zohs*-tahf mn'yeh fspoh-*koh*-yoo
Stop bothering me!	**Odczep się!** *oht*-chehp sh'yeh

Getting Intimate

Can I hug/kiss you?	**Mogę cię przytulić/pocałować?** *moh*-geh ch'yeh pshyh-*too*-leech'/poh-tsah-*woh*-vahch'
Yes.	**Tak.** *tahk*
No.	**Nie.** *n'yeh*
Stop!	**Przestań!** *pshehs*-tahn'
I love you	**Kocham cię** *koh*-hahm ch'yeh

Sexual Preferences

Are you gay?	**Jesteś gejem** m **/lesbijką** f**?** *yehs*-tehsh' *geh*-yehm/ *lehs*-*beey*-kohm
I'm...	**Jestem...** *yehs*-tehm...
heterosexual	**heteroseksualny** m **/heteroseksualna** f *heh*-teh-roh-sehk-soo-*ahl*-nyh/ *heh*-teh-roh-sehk-soo-*ahl*-nah
gay	**gejem** m **/lesbijką** f *geh*-yehm/lehs-*beey*-kohm
bisexual	**biseksualny** m **/biseksualna** f *bee*-sehk-soo-*ahl*-nyh/bee-sehk-soo-*ahl*-nah
Do you like men/women?	**Wolisz mężczyzn/kobiety?** *voh*-leesh mehnzh-*chyhzn*/koh-*byeh*-tyh

For Grammar, see page 166

Leisure Time

Sightseeing

ESSENTIAL

Where's the tourist information office?	**Gdzie jest biuro informacji turystycznej?** *gdj'yeh yehst <u>byoo</u>·roh een·fohr·<u>mah</u>·tsyee too·ryhs·<u>tyhch</u>·nehy*
What are the main points of interest?	**Co tu warto zobaczyć?** *tsoh too <u>vahr</u>·toh zoh·<u>bah</u>·chyhch'*
Are there tours in English?	**Czy są wycieczki po angielsku?** *chyh sohm vyh·<u>ch'yech</u>·kee poh ahn·<u>gyehl</u>·skoo*
Can I have a map/ guide please?	**Czy mogę prosić mapę/przewodnik?** *chyh <u>moh</u>·geh <u>proh</u>·sh'eech' mah·peh/psheh·<u>vohd</u>·n'eek*

While visiting Poland, tourists can enjoy arts and culture throughout the year. Classical music enthusiasts should visit Chopin's birthplace, Żelazowa Wola, during the summer for free outdoor concerts. Historic Cracow features many art galleries and museums, including **Muzeum Narodowe** (National Museum) and **Muzeum Czartoryskich** (Cartoryski Museum). Warsaw, Poland's capital, is home to numerous renowned theaters and concert halls, as well as one of Europe's most beautiful city parks, **Łazienki Królewskie**. During August, the beach town of Sopot entertains music lovers with its International Pop Festival.

Tourist Information

Do you have any information on...?	**Czy ma pan jakieś informacje o...?** *chyh mah pahn <u>yah</u>·kyehsh' een·fohr·<u>mah</u>·tsyeh oh...*
Can you recommend...?	**Czy może pan polecić...?** *chyh <u>moh</u>·zheh pahn poh·<u>leh</u>·ch'eech'...*

a bus tour	**wycieczkę autobusową** *vyh·ch'yehch·keh ahw·toh·boo·soh·wohm*
a boat trip	**rejs statkiem** *rehys staht·kyehm*
an excursion	**wycieczkę** *vyh·ch'yehch·keh*
a sightseeing tour	**wycieczkę po mieście** *vyh·ch'yehch·keh poh myehsh'·ch'yeh*

Most cities and large towns have a tourist information office.
They are usually located in the center of town; some display the
sign **IT** (**informacja turystyczna**). Tourist information can also be
obtained from **Orbis** and **PTTK** (Polish Tourist Organization) offices.
Most bookstores and tourist offices sell road, regional and local maps. Town
maps are displayed on kiosks in major squares and streets and at tourist
information offices.

On Tour

I'd like to go on the excursion to…	**Interesuje mnie wycieczka do…** *een·teh·reh·soo·yeh mn'yeh vyh·ch'yehch·kah doh…*
When's the next tour?	**Kiedy będzie następna wycieczka?** *kyeh·dyh behn·dj'yeh nahs·tehmp·nah vyh·ch'yech·kah*
Are there tours in English?	**Czy są wycieczki po angielsku?** *chyh sohm vyh·ch'yech·kee poh ahn·gyehl·skoo*
Is there an English guide book/audio guide?	**Czy jest przewodnik/audioprzewodnik w języku angielskim?** *chyh yehst pshe·vohd·n'eek/ ahwdyoh·pshe·vohd·n'eek vyehn·zyh·koo ahn·gyehl·skyhm*
What time do we leave/return?	**O której wyruszamy/wracamy?** *oh ktoo·rehy vyh·roo·shah·myh/vrah·tsah·myh*
We'd like to see the…	**Chcielibyśmy zobaczyć…** *hch'yeh·lee·byhsh'·myh zoh·bah·chyhch'…*

Can we stop here...?	**Czy możemy się tu zatrzymać...?** *chyh moh·zheh·myh sh'yeh too zaht·shyh·mahch'...*
to take photos	**żeby zrobić zdjęcia** *zheh·byh zroh·beech' zdyehn·ch'yah*
to buy souvenirs	**żeby kupić pamiątki** *zheh·byh koo·peech' pah·myohnt·kee*
to use the restrooms [toilets]	**żeby skorzystać z toalety** *zheh·byh skoh·zhyhs·tahch' stoh·ah·leh·tyh*
Is it disabled-accessible?	**Czy jest dostęp dla niepełnosprawnych?** *chyh yehst dohs·tehmp dlah n'yeh·pehw·noh·sprahv·nyhh*

For Tickets, see page 19.

Seeing the Sights

Where's...?	**Gdzie jest/są...?** *gdj'yeh yehst/sohm*
the battleground	**pole bitwy** *poh·leh beet·fyh*
the botanical garden	**ogród botaniczny** *oh·groot boh·tah·n'eech·nyh*
the castle	**zamek** *zah·mehk*
the cathedral	**katedra** *kah·teh·drah*
the church	**kościół** *kosh'·ch'yoow*
the downtown area	**centrum** *tsehn·troom*
the fountain	**fontanna** *fohn·tahn·nah*
the library	**biblioteka** *beeb·lyoh·teh·kah*
the market	**bazar** *bah·zahr*
the monument	**pomnik** *pohm·n'eek*
the museum	**muzeum** *moo·zeh·oom*
the old town	**stare miasto** *stah·reh myahs·toh*
the opera house	**opera** *oh·peh·rah*
the palace	**pałac** *pah·wahts*
the park	**park** *pahrk*
the ruins	**ruiny** *roo·ee·nyh*
the shopping area	**centrum handlowe** *tsehn·troom hahn·dloh·veh*

the town square	**rynek** _ryh•nehk_
the town hall	**ratusz** _rah•toosh_
Can you show me on the map?	**Czy może mi pan pokazać na mapie?** _chyh moh•zheh mee pahn poh•kah•zahch' nah mah•pyeh_
It's...	**To jest...** _toh yehst..._
amazing	**niesamowite** _n'yeh•sah•moh•vee•teh_
beautiful	**piękne** _pyehnk•neh_
boring	**nudne** _nood•neh_
interesting	**interesujące** _een•teh•reh•soo•yohn•tseh_
magnificent	**wspaniałe** _vspah•n'yah•weh_
romantic	**romantyczne** _roh•mahn•tyhch•neh_
strange	**dziwne** _dj'eev•neh_
stunning	**olśniewające** _ohl•sh'n'yeh•vah•yohn•tseh_
terrible	**okropne** _ohk•rohp•neh_
ugly	**brzydkie** _bzhyht•kyeh_
I (don't) like it.	**(Nie) Podoba mi się to.** _(n'yeh) poh•doh•bah mee sh'yeh toh_

For Asking Directions, see page 34.

Religious Sites

Where's...?	**Gdzie jest...?** _gdj'yeh yehst_
the cathedral	**katedra** _kah•teh•drah_
the Catholic/ Protestant church	**kościół katolicki/protestancki** _kosh'•ch'yoow kah•toh•lee•tskee/ proh•tehs•tahn•tskee_
the mosque	**meczet** _meh•cheht_
the shrine	**kapliczka** _kah•pleech•kah_
the synagogue	**synagoga** _syh•nah•goh•gah_
What time is mass/ the service?	**O której jest msza/nabożeństwo?** _oh ktoo•rehy yehst mshah/nah•boh•zhehn'•stfoh_

Shopping

ESSENTIAL

Where is the market/ mall [shopping centre]?	**Gdzie jest targ/centrum handlowe?** *gdj'yeh yehst tahrk/tsehn·troom hahn·dloh·veh*
I'm just browsing.	**Tylko się rozglądam.** *tyhl·koh sh'yeh rohz·glohn·dahm*
Can you help me?	**Czy może mi pan pomóc?** *chyh moh·zheh mee pahn poh·moots*
I'm being helped.	**Jestem już obsługiwany m /obsługiwana f.** *yehs·tehm yoosh ohp·swoo·gee·vah·nyh/ ohp·swoo·gee·vah·nah*
How much is this/that?	**Ile to/tamto kosztuje?** *ee·leh toh/tahm·toh kosh·too·yeh*
Can you show me...?	**Może mi pan pokazać...?** *moh·zheh mee pahn poh·kah·zahch'...*
This/That one, please.	**Proszę to/tamto.** *proh·sheh toh/tahm·toh*
That's all, thanks.	**To wszystko, dziękuję.** *toh fshyhs·tkoh dj'yehn·koo·yeh*

Where can I pay?	**Gdzie mogę zapłacić?** *gdj'yeh moh-geh zah-pwah-ch'eech'*
I'll pay in cash/ by credit card.	**Zapłacę gotówką/kartą kredytową.** *zah-pwah-tseh goh-toof-kohm/kahr-tohm kreh-dyh-toh-vohm*
A receipt, please.	**Proszę paragon.** *proh-sheh pah-rah-gohn*

At the Shops

Where is/are...?	**Gdzie jest/są...?** *gdj'yeh yehst/sohm...*
When does...open/ close?	**Od/Do której czynny jest...?** *ohd/doh ktoo-rehy chyhn-nyh yehst...*
the antiques store	**antykwariat** *ahn-tyh-kfah-ryaht*
the bakery	**piekarnia** *pyeh-kahr-n'yah*
the bank	**bank** *bahnk*
the butcher shop	**sklep mięsny** *sklehp myehn-snyh*
the bookstore	**księgarnia** *ksh'yehn-gahr-n'yah*
the camera shop	**sklep fotograficzny** *sklehp foh-toh-grah-feech-nyh*
the clothing store	**sklep odzieżowy** *sklehp oh-dj'yeh-zhoh-vyh*
the delicatessen	**delikatesy** *deh-lee-kah-teh-syh*
the department store	**dom towarowy** *dohm toh-vah-roh-vyh*
the florist	**kwiaciarnia** *kfyah-ch'yahr-n'yah*
the gift shop	**sklep z upominkami** *sklehp zoo-poh-meen-kah-mee*
grocery store	**sklep spożywczy** *sklehp spoh-zhyhf-chyh*
the health food store	**sklep ze zdrową żywnością** *sklehp zeh zdroh-vohm zhyhv-nohsh'-ch'yohm*
the jeweler	**jubiler** *yoo-bee-lehr*
the liquor store [off-licence]	**sklep monopolowy** *sklehp moh-noh-poh-loh-vyh*
market	**bazar** *bah-zahr*
the music store	**sklep muzyczny** *sklehp moo-zyhch-nyh*

the pastry shop	**cukiernia** *tsoo·kyehr·n'yah*
the pharmacy [chemist]	**apteka** *ahp·teh·kah*
the produce [grocery] store	**sklep z artykułami spożywczymi** *sklehp zahr·tyh·koo·wah·mee spoh·zhyhf·chyh·mee*
the shoe store	**sklep obuwniczy** *sklehp oh·boov·n'ee·chyh*
the shopping mall [centre]	**centrum handlowe** *tsehn·troom hahn·dloh·veh*
the souvenir store	**sklep z pamiątkami** *sklehp spahm·yohnt·kah·mee*
the sporting store	**sklep sportowy** *sklehp spohr·toh·vyh*
the supermarket	**supermarket** *soo·pehr·mahr·keht*
the tobacconist	**sklep tytoniowy** *sklehp tyh·toh·n'yoh·vyh*
the newsstand	**kiosk z gazetami** *kyohsk zgah·zeh·tah·mee*
the toy store	**sklep z zabawkami** *sklehp zzah·bahf·kah·mee*

Ask an Assistant

What are the opening hours?	**Jakie są godziny otwarcia?** *yah·kyeh sohm goh·dj'ee·nyh oht·fahr·ch'yah*
Where is/are...?	**Gdzie jest/są...?** *gdj'yeh yehst/sohm...*
the cashier	**kasa** *kah·sah*
the escalators	**schody ruchome** *shoh·dyh roo·hoh·meh*
the elevator [lift]	**winda** *veen·dah*

the fitting room	**przymierzalnia**	pshyh·myeh·_zhahl_·n'yah
the store directory [guide]	**tablica informacyjna**	tah·_blee_·tsah een·fohr·mah·_tsyhy_·nah
Can you help me?	**Czy może mi pan pomóc?**	chyh _moh_·zheh mee pahn _poh_·moots
I'm just looking	**Tylko się rozglądam**	_tyhl_·koh sh'yeh rohz·_glohn_·dahm
I'm being helped.	**Jestem już obsługiwany m/obsługiwana f.**	_yehs_·tehm yoosh ohp·swoo·gee·_vah_·nyh/ ohp·swoo·gee·_vah_·nah
Do you have…?	**Czy mają państwo…?**	chyh _mah_·yohm pahn'·stfoh…
Can you show me…?	**Czy może mi pan pokazać…?**	chyh _moh_·zheh mee pahn poh·_kah_·zahch'…
Can you ship/wrap it?	**Można prosić o wysłanie/opakowanie?**	_mohzh_·nah _proh_·sh'eech' oh vyh·_swah_·n'yeh/oh·pah·koh·_vah_·n'yeh
How much?	**Ile to kosztuje?**	_ee_·leh toh kohsh·_too_·yeh
That's all, thanks.	**To wszystko, dziękuję.**	toh _fshyhst_·koh dj'yehn·_koo_·yeh

For Clothing, see page 124.
For Meals & Cooking, see page 65.
For Souvenirs, see page 130.

YOU MAY HEAR…

Czym mogę służyć? chyhm _moh_·geh _swoo_·zhyhch'	Can I help you?
Chwileczkę. hvee·_lehch_·keh	One moment.
Co podać? tsoh _poh_·dahch'	What would you like?
To wszystko? toh _fshyhst_·koh	Is that all?

YOU MAY SEE...

Zamknięte/otwarte	open/closed
Przerwa śniadaniowa	closed for lunch
Przymierzalnia	fitting room
Kasa	cashier
Płatność tylko gotówką	cash only
Przyjmujemy karty kredytowe	credit cards accepted
Godziny otwarcia	business hours
Wyjście	exit

Personal Preferences

I want something...	**Chciałbym** *m* /**Chciałabym** *f* **coś...** *hch'yahw•byhm/hch'yah•wah•byhm tsohsh'...*
cheap/expensive	**taniego/drogiego** *tah•n'yeh•goh/droh•gyeh•goh*
larger/smaller	**większego/mniejszego** *vyehn•ksheh•goh/ mn'yehy•sheh•goh*
from this region	**miejscowego** *myehy•stsoh•veh•goh*
Around...euros/złotych.	**około ... euro** *oh•koh•woh ... ehw•roh/zwoh•tyhh*
Is it real/fake?	**Czy to jest prawdziwe/sztuczne?** *chyh toh yehst prahv•dj'ee•veh/shtoo•chneh*
Could I see this/that?	**Czy mogę zobaczyć to/tamto?** *chyh moh•geh zoh•bah•chyhch' toh/tahm•toh*
That's not quite what I want.	**To nie to, czego szukam.** *toh n'yeh toh cheh•goh shoo•kahm*
I don't like it.	**To mi się nie podoba.** *toh mee sh'yeh n'yeh poh•doh•bah*
It's too expensive	**To jest za drogie** *toh yehst zah droh•gyeh*
I'd like to think about it.	**Chcę się nad tym zastanowić.** *htseh sh'yeh naht tyhm zahs•tah•noh•veech'*
I'll take it.	**Wezmę to.** *vehz•meh toh*

Paying & Bargaining

How much?	**Ile to kosztuje?** _ee·leh toh kosh·too·yeh_
I'll pay in cash/	**Zapłacę gotówką/kartą kredytową/czekiem**
by credit card/	**podróżnym.** _zah·pwah·tseh goh·toof·kohm/_
by traveler's check.	_kahr·tohm kreh·dyh·toh·vohm/cheh·kyehm_
	pohd·roozh·nyhm
A receipt, please.	**Proszę paragon.** _proh·sheh pah·rah·gohn_
That's too much.	**To za drogo.** _toh zah droh·goh_
I'll give you…	**Dam panu…** _dahm pah·noo…_
I only have…zlotys.	**Mam tylko…złotych.** _mahm tyhl·koh…zwoh·tyhh_
Is that your best price?	**To najniższa cena?** _toh nay·n'eezh·shah tseh·nah_
Can you give me a discount?	**Da mi pan zniżkę?** _dah mee pahn zn'eezh·keh_

For Numbers, see page 171.

YOU MAY HEAR…

Jak chce pan zapłacić? _yahk htseh pahn zah·pwah·ch'eech'_	How are you paying?
Transakcja została odrzucona. _trahn·sahk·tsyah zoh·stah·wah ohd·zhoo·tsoh·nah_	Your credit card has been declined.
Proszę o dowód tożsamości. _proh·sheh oh doh·voot tohzh·sah·moh·sh'ch'ee_	ID, please.
Nie przyjmujemy kart kredytowych. _n'yeh pshyh·ymoo·yeh·myh kahrt kreh·dyh·toh·vyhh_	We don't accept credit cards.
Płatność tylko gotówką. _pwaht·nohsh'ch' tyhl·koh goh·toof·kohm_	Cash only, please.

Cash is the preferred method of paying in stores. Larger stores
and retail chains usually accept major credit cards. Travelers
checks and personal checks are rarely accepted in Poland.

Making a Complaint

I'd like…	**Chciałbym** m /**Chciałabym** f… hch'yahw•byhm/ hch'yah•wah•byhm…
to exchange this	**to wymienić** toh vyh•myeh•n'eech'
to return this	**to oddać** toh ohd•dahch'
a refund	**zwrot pieniędzy** zvroht pyeh•n'ehn•dzyh
to see the manager	**porozmawiać z kierownikiem** poh•rohz•mah•vyahch' skyeh•rohv•n'ee•kyehm
Here's the receipt.	**Oto paragon.** oh•toh pah•rah•gohn

Services

Can you recommend…?	**Czy może pan polecić…?** chyh moh•zheh pahn poh•leh•ch'eech'…
a barber	**fryzjera męskiego** fryh•zyeh•rah mehn•skyeh•goh
a dry cleaner	**pralnię chemiczną** prahl•n'yeh heh•meech•nohm
a hairdresser	**fryzjera** fryh•zyeh•rah
a laundromat [launderette]	**pralnię samoobsługową** prahl•n'yeh sah•moh•ohp•swoo•goh•vohm
a nail salon	**manikiurzystkę** mah•nee•kyoo•zhyhs•tkeh
a spa	**spa** spah
a travel agency	**biuro podróży** byoo•roh pohd•roo•zhyh
Can you…this?	**Może pan to…?** moh•zheh pahn toh…
alter	**poprawić** poh•prah•veech'
clean	**wyczyścić** vyh•chyhsh'•ch'eech'
mend	**załatać** zah•wah•tahch'
press	**wyprasować** vyh•prah•soh•vahch'

| When will it be ready? | **Na kiedy to będzie gotowe?** *nah <u>kyeh</u>•dyh toh <u>behn</u>•dj'yeh goh•<u>toh</u>•veh* |

Hair & Beauty

I'd like an appointment for today/tomorrow.	**Chciałbym** *m* **/Chciałabym** *f* **umówić się na dzisiaj/ jutro.** *<u>hch'yahw</u>•byhm /<u>hch'yah</u>•wah•byhm oo•<u>moo</u>•veech' sh'yeh nah <u>dj'ee</u>•sh'yahy/<u>yoot</u>•roh*
I'd like...	**Poproszę o...** *poh•<u>proh</u>•sheh oh...*
some colour/ highlights	**trochę koloru/pasemka** *<u>troh</u>•heh koh•<u>loh</u>•roo/ pah•<u>sehm</u>•kah*
my hair styled/ blow-dried	**ułożenie/wysuszenie włosów** *oo•woh•<u>zheh</u>•n'yeh/ vyh•soo•<u>sheh</u>•n'yeh <u>vwoh</u>•soof*
a haircut	**strzyżenie** *st•shyh•<u>zheh</u>•n'yeh*
an eyebrow/ bikini wax	**depilację brwi/bikini woskiem** *deh•pee•<u>lahts</u>•yeh brvee/bee•<u>kee</u>•n'ee <u>vohs</u>•kyehm*
a facial	**zabieg na twarz** *<u>zah</u>•byehk nah tfahsh*
a manicure/pedicure	**manicure/pedicure** *<u>mah</u>•n'ee•kyoor/<u>peh</u>•dee•kyoor*
a (sports) massage	**masaż (sportowy)** *<u>mah</u>•sash (spohr•<u>toh</u>•vyh)*
a trim	**podcięcie włosów** *poht•<u>ch'yen</u>•ch'yeh <u>vwoh</u>•soof*
Not too short	**Nie za krótko** *n'yeh zah <u>kroot</u>•koh*
Shorter here	**Krócej tutaj** *<u>kroot</u>•tsehy <u>too</u>•tahy*

Do you offer...?	**Czy prowadzą państwo...?** *chyh proh·vah·dzohm pahn's·tfoh...*
I'd like...	**Poproszę o...** *poh·proh·sheh oh...*
acupuncture	**akupunkturę** *ah·koo·poon·ktoo·reh*
aromatherapy	**aromaterapię** *ah·roh·mah·teh·rah·pyeh*
oxygen treatment	**terapię tlenową** *teh·rah·pyeh tleh·noh·vohm*
Is there a sauna?	**Czy jest sauna?** *chyh yehst sahw·nah*

Throughout Poland, there are many popular health resorts of long-standing tradition (Busko-Zdrój, Konstancin Jeziorna, Duszniki Zdrój, Krynica, Nałęczów, Szczawnica) where the waters are known to have healing qualities. Spas and wellness centers, day and overnight, can be found in large cities and seaside resorts (Jurata, Jastarnia, Łeba, Sopot, Ustka), the lake region (Augustów) and the mountains (Zakopane, Bielsko-Biała). These offer a wide range of high-quality services and are usually relatively expensive.

Antiques

How old is this?	**Ile to ma lat?** *ee·leh toh mah laht*
Do you have anything from the...period?	**Ma pan coś z okresu...?** *mah pahn tsohsh' zoh·kreh·soo...*
Do I have to fill out any forms?	**Czy muszę wypełniać jakiś formularz?** *chyh moo·sheh vyh·pehw·n'yahch' yah·keesh' fohr·moo·lahsh*
Is there a certificate of authenticity?	**Czy to ma świadectwo autentyczności?** *chyh toh mah sh'fyah·dehts·tfoh aw·tehn·tyhch·nohsh'·ch'ee*
Can you ship/wrap it?	**Można prosić o wysłanie/opakowanie tego?** *mohzh·nah proh·sh'eech' oh vyh·swah·n'yeh/ oh·pah·koh·vah·n'yeh teh·goh*

Clothing

I'd like…	**Chciałbym** *m* /**Chciałabym** *f* … *hch'yahw•byhm/ hch'yah•wah•byhm…*
Can I try this on?	**Czy mogę to przymierzyć?** *chyh moh•geh toh pshyh•myeh•zhyhch'*
It doesn't fit.	**To nie pasuje.** *toh n'yeh pah•soo•yeh*
It's too…	**To jest za…** *toh yehst zah…*
big	**duże** *doo•zheh*
small	**małe** *mah•weh*
short	**krótkie** *kroot•kyeh*
long	**długie** *dwoo•gyeh*
tight	**ciasne** *ch'yah•sneh*
loose	**luźne** *loo•zh'neh*
Do you have this in size…?	**Czy jest rozmiar…?** *chyh yehst rohz•myahr…*
Do you have this in a bigger/smaller size?	**Czy są większe/mniejsze rozmiary?** *chyh sohm vyehnk•sheh/mn'yehy•sheh rohz•myah•ryh*

For Numbers, see page 171.

For Clothes & Accessories, see page 126.

YOU MAY HEAR...

Świetnie w tym pan wygląda _sh'vyeht•n'yeh pahn ftyhm wyh•glohn•dah_	That looks great on you.
Jak to pasuje? _yahk toh pah•soo•yeh_	How does it fit?
Nie mamy pana rozmiaru _n'yeh mah•myh pah•nah rohz•myah•roo_	We don't have your size.

YOU MAY SEE...

ODZIEŻ DAMSKA	men's clothing
ODZIEŻ MĘSKA	women's clothing
UBRANIA DLA DZIECI	children's clothing

Colors

I want something...	**Chciałbym** _m_ /**Chciałabym** _f_ **coś w kolorze...** _hch'yahw•byhm_ /_hch'yah•wah•byhm tsohsh' fkoh•loh•zheh..._
beige	**beżowym** _beh•zhoh•vyhm_
black	**czarnym** _chahr•nyhm_
blue	**niebieskim** _n'yeh•byehs•keem_
brown	**brązowym** _brohn•zoh•vyhm_
gray	**szarym** _shah•ryhm_
green	**zielonym** _zh'yeh•loh•nyhm_
olive	**oliwkowym** _oh•leef•koh•vyhm_
orange	**pomarańczowym** _poh•mah•rahn'•choh•vyhm_
pink	**różowym** _roo•zhoh•vyhm_
purple	**fioletowym** _fioh•leh•toh•vyhm_
red	**czerwonym** _chehr•voh•nyhm_

| white | **białym** _byah_•wyhm |
| yellow | **żółtym** _zhoow_•tyhm |

Clothes & Accessories

a backpack	**plecak** _pleh_•tsahk
a bag	**torba** _tohr_•bah
a belt	**pasek** _pah_•sehk
a bikini	**bikini** bee•_kee_•n'ee
a blouse	**bluzka** _bloos_•kah
a bra	**biustonosz** byoos•_toh_•nohsh
briefs [underpants]/	**majtki (for both sexes)/slipy (for men)/**
panties	**figi (for women)** _mahyt_•kee/ _slee_•pyh/ _fee_•gee
a coat (long/short)	**płaszcz/kurtka** pwahshch/_koort_•kah
a dress	**sukienka** soo•_kyehn_•kah
a hat	**kapelusz** kah•_peh_•loosh
a jacket	**marynarka** _m_ **/żakiet** _f_ mah•ryh•_nahr_•kah/ _zhah_•kyeht
jeans	**dżinsy** _dj'een_•syh
pajamas	**piżama** pee•_zhah_•mah
pants [trousers]	**spodnie** _spohd_•n'yeh
pantyhose [tights]	**rajstopy** ray•_stoh_•pyh
a purse [handbag]	**torebka** toh•_rehp_•kah
a raincoat	**płaszcz przeciwdeszczowy** pwahshch psheh•ch'eev•dehsh•_choh_•vyh
a scarf	**szalik** _shah_•leek
a shirt	**koszula** _m_ **/bluzka** _f_ koh•_shoo_•lah /_bloos_•kah
shorts	**szorty** _shohr_•tyh
a skirt	**spódnica** spood•_n'ee_•tsah
socks	**skarpetki** skahr•_peht_•kee
stockings	**pończochy** pohn'•_choh_•hyh
a suit	**garnitur** _m_ **/kostium** _f_ gahr•_n'ee_•toor /_kohs_•tyoom

sunglasses	**okulary przeciwsłoneczne** oh·koo·*lah*·ryh psheh·ch'eef·swoh·*nehch*·neh
a sweater	**sweter** *sfeh*·tehr
a sweatshirt	**bluza** *bloo*·zah
swimming trunks	**kąpielówki** kohm·pyeh·*loof*·kee
a swimsuit	**kostium kąpielowy** kohs·tyoom kohm·pyeh·*loh*·vyh
a T-shirt	**t-shirt** *tee*·shehrt
a tie	**krawat** *krah*·vaht
underwear	**bielizna** byeh·*lee*·znah

Fabric

I'd like…	**Chciałbym** m /**Chciałabym** f **coś…** *hch'yahw*·byhm /*hch'yah*·wah·byhm tsohsh'…
cotton	**z bawełny** zbah·*vehw*·nyh
denim	**z dżinsu** *zdjeen*·soo
lace	**z koronki** skoh·*rohn*·kee
leather	**ze skóry** zeh *skoo*·ryh
linen	**z lnu** z*lnoo
silk	**z jedwabiu** zyehd·*vah*·byoo
wool	**z wełny** *zvehw*·nyh
Is it machine washable?	**Czy można to prać w pralce?** chyh *mohzh*·nah toh prahch' f*prahl*·tseh

Shoes

I'd like…	**Chciałbym** m /**Chciałabym** f… *hch'yahw*·byhm /*hch'yah*·wah·byhm…
high-heeled/ flat shoes	**buty na wysokim obcasie/płaskim obcasie** *boo*·tyh nah vyh·*soh*·keem ohp·*tsah*·sh'yeh/*pwahs*·keem ohp·*tsah*·sh'yeh
boots	**botki** *boht*·kee
loafers	**mokasyny** moh·kah·*syh*·nyh
sandals	**sandały** sahn·*dah*·wyh

shoes	**buty** _boo_•tyh
slippers	**kapcie** _kahp_•ch'yeh
sneakers	**buty sportowe** _boo_•tyh spohr•_toh_•veh
In size…	**Rozmiar…** _rohz_•myahr…

For Numbers, see page 171.

Sizes

small (S)	**mały/S** _mah_•wyh/ehs
medium (M)	**średni/M** _sh'rehd_•n'ee/ehm
large (L)	**duży/L** _doo_•zhyh/ehl
extra large (XL)	**bardzo duży/XL** _bahr_•dzoh _doo_•zhyh/eeks•ehl
petite	**rozmiar petite** _rohz_•myahr peh•_teet_
plus size	**rozmiar plus** _rohz_•myahr ploos

Newsagent & Tobacconist

Do you sell English-language newspapers?	**Czy sprzedają państwo gazety anglojęzyczne?** chyh spsheh•_dah_•yohm pahn'•stfoh gah•_zeh_•tyh anh•gloh•yehn•_zych_•neh
I'd like…	**Poproszę…** poh•_proh_•sheh…
candy	**cukierka/batonik** coo•_kyehr_•kah/bah•_toh_•n'eek
chewing gum	**gumę do żucia** _goo_•meh doh _zhoo_•ch'yah
a chocolate bar	**tabliczkę czekolady** tahb•_leech_•keh cheh•koh•_lah_•dyh
a cigar	**cygaro** tsyh•_gah_•roh
a pack/carton of cigarettes	**paczkę/karton papierosów** _pahch_•keh/_kahr_•tohn pah•pyeh•_roh_•soof
a lighter	**zapalniczkę** zah•pahl•_n'eech_•keh
a magazine	**pismo** _pees_•moh
matches	**zapałki** zah•_pahw_•kee
a newspaper	**gazetę** gah•_zeh_•the
a pen	**długopis** dwoo•_goh_•pees
a postcard	**pocztówkę** pohcz•_toof_•keh

| a road/town map... | **mapę drogową/miasta...** _mah•peh droh•goh•vohm/myah•stah..._ |
| stamps | **znaczki** _znahch•kee_ |

Photography

I'm looking for... camera.	**Szukam...aparatu fotograficznego.** _shoo•kahm... ah•pah•rah•too foh•toh•grah•feech•neh•goh_
an automatic	**automatycznego** _ahw•toh•mah•tych•neh•goh_
a digital	**cyfrowego** _tsyhf•roh•veh•goh_
a disposable	**jednorazowego** _yehd•noh•rah•zoh•veh•goh_
I'd like...	**Poproszę...** _poh•proh•sheh..._
a battery	**baterię** _bah•teh•ryeh_
digital prints	**wydruki zdjęć z aparatu cyfrowego** _vyh•droo•kee zdyehnch' zah•pah•rah•too tsyhf•roh•veh•goh_
a memory card	**kartę pamięci** _kahr•teh pah•myehn'•ch'ee_
Can I print digital photos here?	**Czy mogę tu wydrukować zdjęcia z aparatu cyfrowego?** _chyh moh•geh too vyh•droo•koh•vach' zdyehn'•ch'yah zah•pah•rah•too tsyhf•roh•veh•goh_
When will the photos be ready?	**Na kiedy zdjęcia będą gotowe?** _nah kyeh•dyh zdyehn'•ch'yah behn•dohm goh•toh•veh_

Souvenirs

amber jewelry	**biżuteria z bursztynu** *bee·zhoo·teh·ryah zboor·shtyh·noo*
box of chocolates	**pudełko czekoladek/bombonierka** *poo·dehw·koh cheh·koh·lah·dehk/bohm·boh·n'yehr·kah*
crystal	**kryształ** *kryhsh·tahw*
cut glass	**szlifowane szkło** *shlee·foh·vah·neh shkwoh*
hand-painted eggs	**pisanki** *pee·sahn·kee*
hand-painted wooden box	**ręcznie malowane drewniane pudełko** *rehnch·n'yeh mah·loh·vah·neh drehv·n'yah·neh poo·dehw·koh*
key ring	**breloczek na klucze** *breh·loh·chehk nah kloo·cheh*
Polish vodka	**polska wódka** *pohl·skah voot·kah*
postcard	**pocztówka** *pohch·toof·kah*
poster	**plakat** *plah·kaht*
silver jewelry	**biżuteria ze srebra** *bee·zhoo·teh·ryah zeh sreh·brah*
tapestry	**kilim** *kee·leem*
T-shirt	**t-shirt** *tee·shehrt*
wood carving	**figurka z drewna** *fee·goor·kah zdrehv·nah*
Could I see this/that?	**Czy mogę zobaczyć to/tamto?** *chyh moh·geh zoh·bah·chyhch' toh/tahm·toh*

It's the one in the window/display case.	**To ten na wystawie/w gablocie.** *toh tehn nah vyhs•tah•vyeh/vgah•bloh•ch'yeh*
I'd like…	**Chciałbym m /Chciałabym f …** *hch'yahw•byhm/ hch'yah•wah•byhm…*
a battery	**baterię** *bah•teh•ryeh*
a bracelet	**bransoletkę** *brahn•soh•leht•keh*
a brooch	**broszkę** *brohsh•keh*
earrings	**kolczyki** *kohl•chyh•kee*
a necklace	**naszyjnik** *nah•shyhy•n'eek*
a ring	**pierścionek** *pyehr•sh'ch'yoh•nehk*
a watch	**zegarek** *zeh•gah•rehk*
I'd like…	**Chciałbym m /Chciałabym f coś…** *hch'yahw•byhm /hch'yah•wah•byhm tsohsh'…*
amber	**z bursztynu** *zboor•shtyh•noo*
copper	**z miedzi** *zmyeh•dj'ee*
crystal (quartz)	**z kryształu** *zkryhsh•tah•woo*
diamond	**z brylantami** *zbryh•lahn•tah•mee*
enamel	**z emalii** *zeh•mah•lee*
white/yellow gold	**z białego/żółtego złota** *z byah•weh•goh/ zhoow•teh•goh zwoh•tah*
pearl	**z pereł** *speh•rehw*
pewter	**z cyny** *s•tsyh•nyh*
platinum	**z platyny** *splah•tyh•nyh*
silver	**ze srebra** *zeh sreh•brah*
stainless steel	**ze stali nierdzewnej** *zeh stah•lee n'yeh•rdzehv•nehy*
Is this real?	**Czy to jest prawdziwe?** *chyh toh yehst prahv•dj'ee•veh*
Can you engrave it?	**Można na tym grawerować?** *moh•zhnah nah tyhm grah•veh•roh•vach'*

131

Sport & Leisure

ESSENTIAL

Where's the game?	**Gdzie grają?** _gdj'yeh <u>grah</u>•yohm_
Where's…?	**Gdzie jest…?** _gdj'yeh yehst…_
the beach	**plaża** _plah•zhah_
the park	**park** _pahrk_
the pool	**basen** _bah•sehn_
Is it safe to swim/ dive here?	**Można tu bezpiecznie pływać/skakać?** _<u>mohzh</u>•nah too behs•<u>pyehch</u>•n'yeh <u>pwyh</u>•vahch'/<u>skah</u>•kahch'_
I'd like to rent [hire] golf clubs.	**Chciałbym** _m_ **/Chciałabym** _f_ **wypożyczyć kije golfowe.** _hch'yahw•byhm/hch'yah•wah•byhm fvyh•poh•<u>zhyh</u>•chyhch' <u>kee</u>•yeh gohl•<u>foh</u>•veh_
What's the charge per hour?	**Jaka jest opłata za godzinę?** _<u>yah</u>•kah yehst oh•<u>pwah</u>•tah zah goh•<u>dj'ee</u>•neh_
How far is it to…from here?	**Jak daleko jest stąd do…?** _yahk dah•<u>leh</u>•koh yehst stohnt doh…_
Can you show me on the map?	**Czy może mi pan pokazać na mapie?** _chyh <u>moh</u>•zheh mee pahn poh•<u>kah</u>•zahch' nah <u>mah</u>•pyeh_

Watching Sport

When is...?	**Kiedy jest/są...?** _kyeh•dyh yehst/sohm..._
the basketball game	**mecz koszykówki** _mehch koh•shyh•koof•kee_
the boxing match	**zawody bokserskie** _zah•voh•dyh bohk•sehr•skyeh_
the cycling race	**wyścig rowerowy** _vyhsh'•ch'eeg roh•veh•roh•vyh_
the golf tournament	**zawody golfowe** _zah•voh•dyh gohl•foh•veh_
the soccer [football] game	**mecz piłki nożnej** _mehch peew•kee nohzh•nehy_
the tennis match	**mecz tenisowy** _mehch teh•n'ee•soh•vyh_
Who's playing?	**Kto gra?** _ktoh grah_
Where's...?	**Gdzie jest...?** _gdj'yeh yehst..._
the horsetrack	**tor wyścigów konnych** _tohr vyhsh'•ch'ee•goof kohn•nyhh_
the racetrack	**tor wyścigowy** _tohr vyhsh'•ch'ee•goh•vyh_
the stadium	**stadion** _stah•dyohn_
Where can I place a bet?	**Gdzie można postawić zakład?** _gdj'yeh mohzh•nah pohs•tah•veech' zah•kwaht_

Playing Sport

Where is/are...?	**Gdzie jest/są...?** _gdj'yeh yehst/sohm..._
the golf course	**pole golfowe** _poh•leh gohl•foh•veh_
the gym	**siłownia** _sh'ee•wohv•n'yah_
the park	**park** _pahrk_
the tennis courts	**korty tenisowe** _kohr•tyh teh•n'ee•soh•veh_
How much per...?	**Jaka jest stawka za...?** _yah•kah yehst stah•fkah zah..._
day	**dzień** _dj'yehn'_
hour	**godzinę** _goh•dj'ee•neh_
game	**mecz** _mehch_
round	**turę** _too•reh_

Can I rent [hire]...?	**Czy mogę wypożyczyć...?** *chyh moh•geh vyh•poh•zhyh•chychch'*
golf clubs	**kije do golfa** *kee•yeh doh gohl•fah*
equipment	**sprzęt** *spshehnt*
a racket	**rakietę** *rah•kyeh•teh*

At the Beach/Pool

Where's the beach/pool?	**Gdzie jest plaża/basen?** *gdj'yeh yehst plah•zhah/ bah•sehn*
Is there...?	**Czy jest...?** *chyh yehst...*
a kiddie pool	**brodzik** *broh•dj'eek*
an indoor/ outdoor pool	**basen kryty/odkryty** *bah•sehn kryh•tyh/oht•kryh•tyh*
a lifeguard	**ratownik** *rah•tohv•n'eek*
Is it safe to swim/ dive here?	**Można tu bezpiecznie pływać/skakać?** *mohzh•nah too behs•pyehch•n'yeh pwyh•vach'/skah•kach'*
Is it safe for children?	**Czy jest tu bezpiecznie dla dzieci?** *chyh yehst too behs•pyehch•n'yeh dlah dj'eh•ch'ee*
I'd like to rent [hire]...	**Chciałbym *m* /Chciałabym *f* wypożyczyć...** *hch'yahw•byhm /hch'yah•wah•byhm vyh•poh•zhyh•chychch'...*
a deck chair	**leżak** *leh•zhahk*
diving equipment	**sprzęt do nurkowania** *spshehnt doh noor•koh•vah•n'yah*
a jet-ski	**skuter wodny** *skoo•tehr vohd•nyh*
a motorboat	**motorówkę** *moh•toh•roof•keh*
a rowboat	**łódkę wiosłową** *wood•keh vyohs•woh•vohm*
snorkeling equipment	**sprzęt do nurkowania z fajką** *spshehnt doh noor•koh•vah•n'yah sfahy•kohm*
a surfboard	**deskę surfingową** *dehs•keh soor•feen•goh•vohm*
a towel	**ręcznik** *rehn•chn'eek*

an umbrella	**parasol** *pah·rah·sohl*
waterskis	**narty wodne** *nahr·tyh vohd·neh*
a windsurfer	**deskę windsurfingową** *dehs·keh weend·soor·feen·goh·vohm*
For...hours.	**Na...godzin.** *nah...goh·dj'een*

Poland's sandy Baltic coast beaches are very popular during the summer months. Swim only in places that are marked **plaża strzeżona** (supervised beach) and have a **ratownik** (lifeguard); be sure to obey safety notices. The Mazury Lake District in the north-eastern part of Poland and the Greater Poland Lake District in the north-west are popular tourist destinations, especially for water sports lovers (swimming, sailing, windsurfing, fishing, diving and canoeing).

Winter Sports

A lift pass for a day/ five days, please.	**Poproszę jednodniowy/pięciodniowy skipass.** *poh·proh·sheh yehd·noh·dn'yoh·vyh/ pyehn'·ch'yoh·dn'yoh·vyh skee·pahs*
I'd like to rent [hire]...	**Chciałbym m /Chciałabym f wypożyczyć...** *hch'yahw·byhm/hch'yah·wah·byhm fvyh·poh·zhyh·chyhch'...*
boots	**buty narciarskie** *boo·tyh nahr·ch'yahr·skyeh*
cross-country skis	**biegówki** *byeh·goof·kee*
a helmet	**kask** *kahsk*
poles	**kijki** *keey·kee*
skates	**łyżwy** *wyhzh·vyh*
skis	**narty** *nahr·tyh*
a snowboard	**deskę snowboardową** *dehs·keh snohw·bohr·doh·vohm*
snowshoes	**rakiety śnieżne** *rah·kyeh·tyh sh'n'yehzh·neh*

These are too big/small.	**Te są za duże/małe.** *teh sohm zah doo•zheh/ mah•weh*
Are there ski/ snowboard lessons?	**Czy jest nauka jazdy na nartach/snowboardzie?** *chyh yehst nah•oo•kah yahz•dyh nah nahr•tahh/ snohw•bohr•dj'yeh*
I'm a beginner.	**Jestem początkujący m /początkująca f.** *yehs•tehm poh•chohn•tkoo•yohn•tsyh/ poh•chohn•tkoo•yohn•tsah*
I'm experienced.	**Jestem zaawansowany m /zaawansowana f.** *yehs•tehm zah•ah•vahn•soh•vah•nyh/ zah•ah•vahn•soh•vah•nah*
A trail [piste] map, please.	**Poproszę mapę tras.** *poh•proh•sheh mah•peh trahs*

There are many ski resorts in the southern part of Poland, the most popular being Zakopane, Szczyrk and Wisła. The high Tatra Mountains offer excellent downhill skiing, and there are plenty of skiing opportunities on the lower slopes of many other mountains.

YOU MAY SEE...

WYCIĄG	drag lift
KOLEJKA LINOWA/GONDOLA	cable car/gondola
WYCIĄG KRZESEŁKOWY	chair lift
TRASA ŁATWA	novice
TRASA TRUDNA	intermediate
TRASA BARDZO TRUDNA	expert
TRASA ZAMKNIĘTA	trail [piste] closed
UWAGA LAWINY	caution, avalanches

Out in the Country

I'd like a map of…	**Poproszę mapę…**	poh·_proh_·sheh _mah_·peh…
this region	**tego regionu**	_teh_·goh reh·_gyoh_·noo
the walking routes	**tras pieszych**	trahs pieh·shyhh
the bike routes	**szlaków rowerowych**	_shlah_·koof roh·veh·_roh_·vyhh
the trails	**szlaków**	_shlah_·koof
Is it far?	**Czy to daleko?**	chyh toh dah·_leh_·koh
Is it easy/difficult?	**Czy to łatwa/trudna trasa?**	chyh toh _wah_·tvah/ _troo_·dnah _trah_·sah
Is it steep?	**Jest stromo?**	yehst _stroh_·moh
How far is it to…?	**Jak daleko jest do…?**	yahk dah·_leh_·koh yehst doh
I'm lost.	**Zgubiłem m /Zgubiłam f się.**	zgoo·_bee_·wehm/ zgoo·_bee_·wahm sh'yeh
Where's…?	**Gdzie jest…?**	gdj'yeh yehst…
the bridge	**most**	mohst
the cave	**jaskinia**	yahs·_kee_·n'yah
the cliff	**klif**	kleef
the farm	**gospodarstwo**	goh·spoh·_dahr_·stvoh
the field	**pole**	_poh_·leh
the forest	**las**	lahs
the lake	**jezioro**	yeh·_zh'yoh_·roh

the mountain	**góra** _goo•rah_
the national park	**park narodowy** _pahrk nah•roh•<u>doh</u>•vyh_
the nature reserve	**rezerwat przyrody** _reh•<u>zehr</u>•vaht pshyh•<u>roh</u>•dyh_
the overlook [viewpoint]	**punkt widokowy** _poonkt vee•doh•<u>koh</u>•vyh_
the park	**park** _pahrk_
the path	**ścieżka** _<u>sh'ch'yesh</u>•kah_
the peak	**szczyt** _sh•chyht_
the picnic area	**pole piknikowe** _<u>poh</u>•leh peek•n'ee•<u>koh</u>•veh_
the pond	**staw** _stahv_
the river	**rzeka** _<u>zheh</u>•kah_
the sea	**morze** _<u>moh</u>•zheh_
the (thermal) spring	**(gorące) źródło** _(goh•<u>rohn</u>•tseh) <u>zh'rood</u>•woh_
the stream	**strumień** _<u>stroo</u>•myehn'_
the valley	**dolina** _doh•<u>lee</u>•nah_
the vineyard	**winnica** _veen•<u>nee</u>•tsah_
the waterfall	**wodospad** _voh•<u>dohs</u>•paht_

Going Out

ESSENTIAL

What is there to do at night?	**Co można robić wieczorami?**	*tsoh mohzh·nah roh·beech' vyeh·choh·rah·mee*
Do you have a program of events?	**Czy jest program imprez?**	*chyh yehst proh·grahm eem·prehs*
What's playing at the movies [cinema] today?	**Co dzisiaj grają w kinie?**	*tsoh dj'ee·sh'yay grah·yohm fkee·n'yeh*
Where's...?	**Gdzie jest...?**	*gdj'yeh yehst...*
the downtown area	**centrum**	*tsehn·troom*
the bar	**bar**	*bahr*
the dance club	**dyskoteka**	*dyhs·koh·teh·kah*

Entertainment

Can you recommend...?	**Czy może pan polecić...?**	*chyh moh·zheh pahn poh·leh·ch'eech'...*
a concert	**koncert**	*kohn·tsehrt*
a movie	**film**	*feelm*
an opera	**operę**	*oh·peh·reh*
a play	**sztukę**	*shtoo·keh*

Most hotels will have some information available in English about events around town. There are also culture magazines, such as **Kalejdoskop Kulturalny** (Cultural Kaleidoscope), which have weekly events listings, often provided in Polish and English. These are available at newsstands and bookstores.

When does it start/end?	**Kiedy to się zaczyna/kończy?** _kyeh•dyh toh sh'yeh_
	zah•chyh•nah/kohn'•chyh
I like...	**Lubię...** _loo•byeh..._
classical music	**muzykę poważną** _moo•zyh•keh poh•vahzh•nohm_
folk music	**muzykę ludową** _moo•zyh•keh loo•doh•vohm_
jazz	**jazz** _djehz_
pop music	**pop** _pohp_
rap	**rap** _rahp_
What's the dress code?	**Jaki strój obowiązuje?** _yah•kee strooy_
	oh•boh•vyohn•zoo•yeh

For Tickets, see page 19.

YOU MAY HEAR...

Prosimy o wyłączenie telefonów komórkowych. _proh•shee•myh oh vyh•wohn•cheh•n'yeh teh•leh•foh•noof koh•moor•koh•vyhh_

Turn off your cell [mobile] phones, please.

Nightlife

What is there to do at night?	**Co można robić wieczorami?** _tsoh mohzh•nah roh•beech' vyeh•choh•rah•mee_
Can you recommend...?	**Czy może pan polecić...?** _chyh moh•zheh pahn poh•leh•ch'eech'..._
a bar	**bar** _bahr_
a cabaret	**kabaret** _kah•bah•reht_
a casino	**kasyno** _kah•syh•noh_
a dance club	**dyskotekę** _dyhs•koh•teh•keh_

a gay club	**klub dla gejów**	kloop dlah <u>geh</u>•yoof
a jazz club	**klub jazzowy**	kloop djeh•<u>zoh</u>•vyh
a club with Polish music	**klub z polską muzyką**	kloop <u>spohls</u>•kohm moo•<u>zyh</u>•kohm
Is there live music?	**Czy grają muzykę na żywo?**	chyh grah•yohm moo•<u>zyh</u>•keh nah <u>zhyh</u>•voh
How do I get there?	**Jak tam dotrzeć?**	yahk tahm <u>doh</u>•tshehch'
Is there a cover charge?	**Czy płaci się za wstęp?**	Chyh <u>pwah</u>•ch'ee sh'yeh zah vstehmp
Let's go dancing.	**Chodźmy potańczyć.**	<u>hohch'</u>•myh poh•<u>tahn'</u>•chyhch'
Is this area safe at night?	**Czy ta okolica jest bezpieczna w nocy?**	chyh tah oh•kho•lee•tsah yehst behs•py'eh•chnah vnoh•tsyh

For The Dating Game, see page 107.

Dyskoteki (dance clubs) are popular throughout Poland. These feature a variety of music: dance, jazz, pop, etc. Prices are reasonable and many venues offer student discounts. At popular dance clubs you may need to make a reservation in advance.

Special Requirements

Business Travel

ESSENTIAL

I'm here on business.	**Przyjechałem** *m* **/Przyjechałam** *f* **tutaj służbowo.** *pshyh·yeh·hah·wehm/pshyh·yeh·hah·wahm too·tahy swoozh·boh·voh*
Here's my business card.	**To moja wizytówka.** *toh moh·yah vee·zyh·toof·kah*
Can I have your card?	**Mogę prosić o pana wizytówkę?** *moh·geh proh·sh'eech' oh pah·nah vee·zyh·toof·keh*
I have a meeting with…	**Mam spotkanie z…** *mahm spoht·kah·n'yeh z…*
Where's…?	**Gdzie jest…?** *gdj'yeh yehst…*
the business center	**centrum biznesowe** *tsehn·troom beez·neh·soh·veh*
the convention hall	**sala konferencyjna** *sah·lah kohn·feh·rehn·tsyhy·nah*
the meeting room	**sala spotkań** *sah·lah spoht·kahn'*

On Business

I'm here to attend…	**Przyjechałem** *m* **/Przyjechałam** *f* **na…** *pshyh·yeh·hah·wehm/pshyh·yeh·hah·wahm nah…*
a seminar	**seminarium** *seh·mee·nah·ryoom*
a conference	**konferencję** *kohn·feh·rehn·tsyeh*
a meeting	**spotkanie** *spoht·kah·n'yeh*
My name is…	**Nazywam się…** *nah·zyh·vahm sh'yeh…*
May I introduce my colleague…	**Proszę pozwolić mi przedstawić kolegę…** *proh·sheh pohz·voh·leech' mee pshet·stah·veech' koh·leh·geh…*
Pleasure to meet you.	**Miło mi pana poznać.** *mee·woh mee pah·nah pohz·nahch'*
I have a meeting with…	**Mam spotkanie z…** *mahm spoht·kah·n'yeh z…*

I have an appointment with…	**Jestem umówiony z…** _yehs_·tehm oo·moo·_vyoh_·nyh z…
I'm sorry I'm late.	**Przepraszam za spóźnienie.** psheh·_prah_·shahm zah spoozh'·_n'yeh_·n'yeh
I'd like an interpreter.	**Proszę o tłumacza.** _proh_·sheh oh twoo·_mah_·chah
You can contact me at the…Hotel.	**Można się ze mną kontaktować w hotelu…** _moh_·znah sh'yeh zeh mnohm kohn·tahk·_toh_·vach' f hoh·_teh_·loo…
I'm here until…	**Zostaję tu do…** zohs·_tah_·yeh too doh…
I need to…	**Muszę…** _moo_·sheh…
make a call	**zadzwonić** zah·_dzvoh_·n'eech'
make a photocopy	**zrobić ksero** _zroh_·beech' _kseh_·roh
send an e-mail	**wysłać e-mail** _vyh_·swahch' _ee_·meyl
send a fax	**wysłać fax** _vyh_·swahch' fahks
send a package (for next day delivery)	**wysłać paczkę (pocztą kurierską)** _vyh_·swahch' _pahch_·keh (_pohch_·tohm koor·_yehr_·skohm)

For Communications, see page 47.

Business people who meet for the first time shake hands and share their first names and surnames. Avoid clasping the hand of your partner with both hands. It is an accepted custom to exchange business cards at the first meeting. For subsequent meetings simply say: **dzień dobry/dobry wieczór** (hello/good evening) and shake hands. If a woman and a man meet, she is supposed to reach out her hand first. However, if two business people occupy different positions, it is always the senior one who reaches out his/her hand first.

YOU MAY HEAR...

Czy jest pan umówiony na spotkanie?
chyh yehst pahn oo·moo·vyoh·nyh nah spoht·kah·n'yeh

Do you have an appointment?

Z kim? *skeem*

With whom?

Jest na zebraniu. *yehst nah zehb·rah·n'yoo*

He/She is in a meeting.

Proszę chwilę poczekać. *proh·sheh hvee·leh poh·cheh·kahch'*

One moment, please.

Proszę usiąść. *proh·sheh oo·sh'ohn'sh'ch'*

Have a seat.

Dziękuję za przybycie. *dj'yehn·koo·yeh zah pshyh·byh·ch'yeh*

Thank you for coming.

Traveling with Children

ESSENTIAL

Is there a discount for children?	**Czy jest zniżka dla dzieci?** *chyh yehst zn'eezh•kah dlah dj'yeh•ch'ee*
Can you recommend a babysitter?	**Czy może pan polecić opiekunkę do dzieci?** *chyh moh•zheh pahn poh•leh•ch'eech' oh•pyeh•koon•keh doh dj'yeh•ch'ee*
Do you have a child's seat/highchair?	**Mają państwo krzesełko dla dziecka/wysokie krzesełko?** *mah•yohm pahn'•stfoh ksheh•seh•wkoh dlah dj'yeh•tskah/vyh•soh•kyeh ksheh•seh•wkoh*
Where can I change the baby?	**Gdzie mogę przewinąć dziecko?** *gdj'yeh moh•geh psheh•vee•nohn'ch' dj'yehts•koh*

Out & About

Can you recommend something for kids?	**Czy może pan polecić coś dla dzieci?** *chyh moh•zheh pahn poh•leh•ch'eech' tsohsh' dlah dj'yeh•ch'ee*
Where's…?	**Gdzie jest…?** *gdj'yeh yehst…*
the amusement park	**wesołe miasteczko** *veh•soh•weh myahs•teh•chkoh*
the arcade	**salon gier** *sah•lohn gyehr*
the kiddie [paddling] pool	**brodzik** *broh•dj'eek*
the park	**park** *pahrk*
the playground	**plac zabaw** *plahts zah•bahf*
the zoo	**zoo** *zoh•oh*
Are children allowed?	**Czy można wchodzić z dziećmi?** *chyh mohzh•nah fhoh•dj'eech' zdj'yehch'•mee*
Is it safe for kids?	**Czy to jest bezpieczne dla dzieci?** *chyh toh yehst behs•pyehch•neh dlah dj'yeh•ch'ee*
Is it suitable for… year olds?	**Czy to jest odpowiednie dla…-latków?** *chyh toh yehst oht•poh•vyehd•n'yeh dlah…-laht•koof*

For Numbers, see page 171.

YOU MAY HEAR…

Jakie słodkie! *yah•kyeh swoht•kyeh*	How cute!
Jak ma na imię? *yahk mah nah ee•myeh*	What's his/her name?
Ile ma lat? *ee•leh mah laht*	How old is he/she?

Baby Essentials

Do you have…?	**Czy mają państwo…?** *chyh mah·yohm pahn'·stfoh…*	
a baby bottle	**butelkę ze smoczkiem** *boo·tehl·keh zeh smohch·kyehm*	
baby wipes	**wilgotne chusteczki pielęgnacyjne** *veel·goht·neh hoos·tehch·kee pyeh·lehn·gnah·tsyhy·neh*	
a car seat	**fotelik samochodowy** *foh·teh·leek sah·moh·hoh·doh·vyh*	
a child's seat/ highchair	**krzesełko dla dziecka/wysokie krzesełko** *ksheh·seh·wkoh dlah dj'yeh·tskah/vyh·soh·kyeh ksheh·seh·wkoh*	
a crib/cot	**łóżko składane/łóżeczko dziecięce** *woo·shkoh skwah·dah·neh/woo·zhehch·koh dj'yeh·ch'ehn·tseh*	
diapers [nappies]	**pieluszki** *pyeh·loosh·kee*	
a pacifier [dummy]	**smoczek** *smoh·chehk*	
a playpen	**kojec** *koh·yehts*	
a stroller [pushchair]	**wózek spacerowy** *voo·zehk spah·tseh·roh·vyh*	
Can I breastfeed the baby here?	**Czy mogę tutaj karmić dziecko piersią?** *chyh moh·geh too·tay kahr·meech' dj'yehts·koh pyehr·sh'yohm*	

| Where can I change the baby? | **Gdzie mogę przewinąć dziecko?** *gdj'yeh moh•geh psheh•vee•nohn'ch' dj'yehts•koh* |

For Dining with Children, see page 62.

Babysitting

Can you recommend a babysitter?	**Czy może pan polecić opiekunkę do dzieci?** *chyh moh•zheh pahn poh•leh•ch'eech' oh•pyeh•koon•keh doh dj'yeh•ch'ee*
What's the charge?	**Jaka jest opłata?** *yah•kah yehst oh•pwah•tah*
I'll be back by…	**Przyjdę za…** *pshyhy•deh zah…*
I can be reached at…	**Można do mnie dzwonić na numer…** *moh•zhnah doh mn'yeh dzvoh•n'eech' nah noo•mehr…*

For Time, see page 173.

Health & Emergency

Can you recommend a pediatrician?	**Czy może pan polecić pediatrę?** *chyh moh•zheh pahn poh•leh•ch'eech' peh•dyaht•reh*
My child is allergic to…	**Moje dziecko ma uczulenie na…** *moh•yeh dj'yeh•tskoh mah oo•choo•leh•n'yeh nah…*
My child is missing.	**Moje dziecko się zgubiło.** *moh•yeh dj'yeh•tskoh sh'yeh zgoo•bee•woh*
Have you seen a boy/girl?	**Czy widział pan chłopca/dziewczynkę?** *chyh vee•dj'yahw pahn hwohp•tsah/dj'yehv•chyhn•keh*

For Meals & Cooking, see page 65.

For Health, see page 156.

For Police, see page 154.

Disabled Travelers

ESSENTIAL

Is there…?	**Czy jest…?** *chyh yehst…*
access for the disabled	**dostęp dla niepełnosprawnych** <u>*dohs*</u>*·tehmp dlah n'yeh·pehw·noh·<u>sprahv</u>·nyhh*
a wheelchair ramp	**podjazd dla wózków inwalidzkich** <u>*pohd*</u>*·yahst dlah* <u>*voos*</u>*·koof een·vah·<u>leets</u>·keeh*
a disabled-accessible toilet	**toaleta dla niepełnosprawnych** *toh·ah·<u>leh</u>·tah dlah n'yeh·pew·noh·<u>sprahv</u>·nyhh*
I need…	**Potrzebuję…** *poh·tsheh·<u>boo</u>·yeh…*
assistance	**pomocy** *poh·<u>moh</u>·tsyh*
an elevator [lift]	**windy** <u>*veen*</u>*·dyh*
a ground-floor room	**pokoju na parterze** *poh·<u>koh</u>·yoo nah pahr·<u>teh</u>·zheh*

Asking for Assistance

I'm disabled.	**Jestem nepełnosprawny** *m* /**niepełnosprawna** *f.* <u>*yehs*</u>*·tehm n'yeh·pehw·noh·<u>sprahv</u>·nyh/ n'yeh·pehw·noh·<u>sprahv</u>·nah*
I'm deaf.	**Jestem głuchy** *m* /**głucha** *f.* <u>*yehs*</u>*·tehm* <u>*gwoo*</u>*·hyh/* <u>*gwoo*</u>*·hah*
I'm visually/hearing impaired.	**Niedowidzę./Niedosłyszę.** *n'yeh·doh·<u>vee</u>·dzeh/ n'yeh·doh·<u>swyh</u>·sheh*
I'm unable to walk far/use the stairs.	**Nie mogę dużo chodzić/chodzić po schodach.** *n'yeh <u>moh</u>·geh <u>doo</u>·zhoh hoh·dj'eech'/<u>hoh</u>·dj'eech' poh s·<u>hoh</u>·dahh*
Can I bring my wheelchair?	**Czy mogę być na wózku inwalidzkim?** *chyh <u>moh</u>·geh byhch' nah <u>voos</u>·koo een·vah·<u>leets</u>·keem*

Are guide dogs permitted?	**Czy mogę być z psem przewodnikiem?** *chyh moh•geh byhch' spsehm psheh•vohd•n'ee•kyem*
Can you help me?	**Czy może mi pan pomóc?** *chyh moh•zheh mee pahn poh•moots*
Please open/hold the door.	**Proszę otworzyć/przytrzymać drzwi.** *proh•sheh oht•foh•zhyhch'/pshyh•tshyh•mahch' djvee*

For Emergencies, see page 153.

In an
Emergency

Emergencies

ESSENTIAL

Help!	**Pomocy!** _poh_•_moh_•tsyh
Go away!	**Proszę odejść!** _proh_•sheh _oh_•deysh'ch'
Leave me alone!	**Zostaw mnie w spokoju!** _zoh_•stahf mn'yeh fspoh•_koh_•yoo
Stop thief!	**Łapać złodzieja!** _wah_•pach' zwoh•_dj'yeh_•yah
Get a doctor!	**Wezwijcie lekarza!** vez•_veey_•ch'yeh leh•_kah_•zhah
Fire!	**Pali się!** _pah_•lee sh'yeh
I'm lost.	**Zgubiłem się** _m_ /**Zgubiłam się** _f._ zgoo•_bee_•wehm sh'yeh/zgoo•_bee_•wahm sh'yeh
Can you help me?	**Czy może mi pan pomóc?** chyh _moh_•zheh mee pahn _poh_•moots

YOU MAY HEAR...

Proszę wypełnić ten formularz. _proh_•sheh vyh•_pehw_•n'eech' tehn fohr•_moo_•lash'
Please fill out this form.

Poproszę dowód tożsamości. poh•_proh_•sheh _doh_•voot tohsh's•sah•_mohsh'_•ch'ee
Your identification, please.

Gdzie/Kiedy to się stało? gdj'eh/_kyeh_•dyh toh sh'yeh _stah_•woh
When/Where did it happen?

Jak on/ona wygląda? yahk ohn/_oh_•nah vyh•_glohn_•dah
What does he/she look like?

Proszę tu poczekać. _proh_•sheh too poh•_cheh_•kahch'
Please wait here.

Jak można się z panem skontaktować? yahk _moh_•zhnah sh'yeh _spah_•nehm skohn•tahk•_toh_•vahch'
How may we contact you?

Police

ESSENTIAL

Call the police!	**Wezwijcie policję!** *vez-veey-ch'yeh poh-leets-yeh*
Where's the police station?	**Gdzie jest komisariat?** *gdj'yeh yehst koh-mee-sahr-yaht*
There has been an accident/attack.	**Zdarzył się wypadek/napad.** *zdah-zhyhw sh'yeh vyh-pah-dehk/nah-paht*
My child is missing.	**Moje dziecko się zgubiło.** *moh-yeh dj'yeh-tskoh sh'yeh zgoo-bee-woh*
I need...	**Potrzebuję...** *poh-tsh'eh-boo-yeh...*
an interpreter	**tłumacza** *twoo-mah-chah*
to contact my lawyer	**skontaktować się z moim prawnikiem** *skohn-tah-ktoh-vahch' sh'yeh zmoh-eem prah-vn'ee-kyehm*
to make a phone call	**zatelefonować** *zah-teh-leh-foh-noh-vach'*
I'm innocent.	**Jestem niewinny** *m* **/niewinna** *f.* *yeh-stehm n'yeh-veen-nyh/n'yeh-veen-nah*
It was an accident.	**To był wypadek.** *toh byhw vyh-pah-dehk*

Crime & Lost Property

I want to report...	**Chcę zgłosić...** *htseh zgwoh-sh'eech'...*
a mugging	**napad** *nah-paht*
a rape	**gwałt** *gvahwt*
a theft	**kradzież** *krah-djyesh*
I've been robbed/ mugged.	**Okradli/Napadli mnie.** *oh-krah-dlee/nah-pah-dlee mn'yeh*

I've lost my...	**Zgubiłem...m /Zgubiłam...f** *zgoo•bee•wehm... / zgoo•bee•wahm...*
My...has been stolen.	**Ukradli mi...** *oo•krah•dlee mee...*
luggage	**bagaż** *bah•gahsh*
backpack [rucksack]	**plecak** *pleh•tsahk*
bicycle	**rower** *roh•vehr*
camera	**aparat fotograficzny** *ah•pah•raht foh•toh•grah•feech•nyh*
video camera	**kamerę** *kah•meh•reh*
(rental [hire]) car	**(wynajęty) samochód** *(vyh•nah•yen•tyh) sah•moh•hoot*
laptop	**laptop** *lahp•tohp*
credit card	**kartę kredytową** *kahr•teh kreh•dyh•toh•vohm*
cell [mobile] phone	**komórkę** *koh•moor•keh*
jewelry	**biżuterię** *bee•zhoo•tehr•yeh*
money	**pieniądze** *pyeh•n'yohn•dzeh*
passport	**paszport** *pahsh•pohrt*
purse [handbag]	**torebkę** *toh•rehp•keh*
travelers checks	**czeki podróżne** *cheh•kee pohd•roozh•neh*
wallet	**portfel** *pohrt•fehl*
I need a police report.	**Muszę mieć raport z policji.** *moo•sheh myehch' rah•pohrt spoh•leets•yee*
Where is the British/ American/Irish embassy?	**Gdzie jest ambasada brytyjska/amerykańska/ irlandzka?** *gdj'yeh yehst ahm•bah•sah•dah bryh•tyhy•skah/ ah•meh•ryh•kahn'•skah eer•lahntskah*

155

In an emergency, dial: **112** for the police
998 for the fire brigade
999 for the ambulance.

Health

ESSENTIAL

I'm sick [ill].	**Jestem chory m /chora f.** *yeh-stehm hoh-ryh / hoh-rah*
I don't feel well.	**Źle się czuję.** *zh'leh sh'yeh choo-yeh*
Is there an English-speaking doctor?	**Czy jest tu lekarz mówiący po angielsku?** *chyh yehst too leh-kahsh moo-vyohn-tsyh poh ahn-gyehls-koo*
It hurts here.	**Boli mnie tutaj.** *boh-lee mn'yeh too-tay*
I have a stomachache.	**Boli mnie brzuch.** *boh-lee mn'yeh bzhooh*

Finding a Doctor

Can you recommend a doctor/dentist?	**Czy może pan polecić lekarza/dentystę?** *chyh moh-zheh pahn poh-leh-ch'eech' leh-kah-zhah/ dehn-tyh-steh*
Could the doctor come to see me here?	**Czy lekarz może przyjść mnie zbadać tutaj?** *chyh leh-kash moh-zheh pshyhysh'ch' mn'yeh zbah-dach' too-tay*

I need an English-speaking doctor.	**Potrzebuję lekarza mówiącego po angielsku.** *poht•sheh•boo•yeh leh•kah•zhah moo•vyohn•tseh•goh poh ahn•gyehls•koo*
What are the office [surgery] hours?	**Jakie są godziny przyjęć?** *yahk•yeh sohm goh•dj'ee•nyh pshyh•yehnch'*
Can I make an appointment...?	**Czy mogę zamówić wizytę...?** *chyh moh•geh zah•moo•veech' vee•zyh•teh...*
for today	**na dzisiaj** *nah dj'ee•sh'yahy*
for tomorrow	**na jutro** *nah yoo•troh*
as soon as possible	**na jak najbliższy termin** *nah yahk nahy•bleesh•shyh tehr•meen*
It's urgent.	**To jest pilne.** *toh yest peel•neh*
It's an emergency.	**To nagły wypadek.** *toh nah•gwyh vyh•pah•dehk*

Symptoms

I'm...	**Mam...** *mahm...*
bleeding	**krwotok** *krfoh•tohk*
constipated	**zaparcie** *zah•pahr•ch'yeh*
dizzy	**zawroty głowy** *zah•vroh•tyh gwoh•vyh*
nauseous	**mdłości** *mdwosh'•ch'ee*
I'm vomiting.	**Wymiotuję.** *vyh•myoh•too•yeh*
It hurts here.	**Boli mnie tutaj.** *boh•lee mn'yeh too•tay*
I have...	**Mam...** *mahm...*
an allergic reaction	**reakcję alergiczną** *reh•ahk•tsyeh ah•lehr•geech•nohm*
chest pain	**bóle w klatce piersiowej** *boo•leh f klaht•tseh pyehr•sh'yoh•vey*
a fever	**gorączkę** *goh•rohnch•keh*
pain	**bóle** *boo•leh*
a rash	**wysypkę** *vyh•syhp•keh*
a sprain	**zwichnięcie** *zvee•hn'yehn'•ch'yeh*

some swelling	**opuchliznę** oh‑poo‑_hleez_‑neh
sunstroke	**udar słoneczny** _oo_‑dahr swoh‑_nehch_‑nyh
I have…	**Boli mnie…** _boh_‑lee mn'yeh…
an earache	**ucho** _oo_‑hoh
a stomachache	**brzuch** bzhooh
a headache	**głowa** _gwoh_‑vah
I've been sick for…days.	**Źle się czuję od…dni.** zh'leh sh'yeh _choo_‑yeh oht…dn'yee

For Numbers, see page 171.

Conditions

I'm…	**Mam…** _mahm_…
anemic	**anemię** ah‑_neh_‑myeh
asthmatic	**astmę** _ahst_‑meh
diabetic	**cukrzycę** tsook‑_shyh_‑tseh
epileptic	**Mam padaczkę** mahm pah‑_dah_‑chkeh
I'm allergic to antibiotics/ penicillin.	**Mam uczulenie na antybiotyki/penicylinę.** Mahm oo‑choo‑_leh_‑n'yeh nah ahn‑tyh‑_byoh_‑tyh‑kee/ peh‑nee‑tsyh‑_lee_‑neh
I have arthritis.	**Mam artretyzm.** mahm ahr‑_treh_‑tyhsm
I have high/low blood pressure.	**Mam wysokie/niskie ciśnienie.** mahm vyh‑_soh_‑kyeh/_nees_‑kyeh ch'eesh'‑_n'yeh_‑n'yeh
I have a heart condition.	**Choruję na serce.** hoh‑_roo_‑yeh na _sehr_‑tseh
I'm on…	**Zażywam…** zah‑_zhyh_‑vahm…

For Meals & Cooking, see page 65.

YOU MAY HEAR...

W czym problem? *fchyhm proh•blehm*

Gdzie boli? *gdj'yeh boh•lee*

Czy boli tutaj? *chyh boh•lee too•tay*

Czy przyjmuje pan regularnie leki?
*chyh pshyhy•moo•yeh pahn
reh•goo•lahr•n'yeh leh•kee*

Czy jest pan na coś uczulony? *chyh yehst
pahn nah tsosh' oo•choo•loh•nyh*

Proszę otworzyć usta. *proh•sheh
oht•foh•zhyhch' oo•stah*

Oddychać głęboko. *ohd•dyh•hach'
gwehm•boh•koh*

Pójdzie pan do szpitala. *pooy•dj'yeh pahn
doh shpee•tah•lah*

What's wrong?

Where does it hurt?

Does it hurt here?

Are you on medication?

Are you allergic to anything?

Please open your mouth.

Breathe deeply.

You must go to the hospital.

Treatment

Do I need a prescription/ medicine?	**Czy potrzebuję lekarstwa/recepty?** *chyh poh•tzheh•boo•yeh leh•kahrs•tfah/ reh•tsehp•tyh*
Can you prescribe a generic drug [unbranded medication]?	**Czy mogę prosić o przepisanie leku generycznego [niemarkowego]** *chyh moh•geh proh•sh'eech' oh psh'eh•pee•sah•nyeh leh•koo geh•neh•ryhch•neh•goh (n'ye•mahr•koh•veh•goh)*
Where can I get it?	**Gdzie to mogę dostać?** *Gdj'yeh toh moh•geh doh•stahch'*

For Pharmacy, see page 162.

Hospital

Please notify my family.	**Proszę zawiadomić moją rodzinę.** _proh·sheh zah·vyah·doh·meech' moh·yohm roh·djee·neh_
I'm in pain.	**Boli mnie.** _boh·lee mn'yeh_
I need a doctor/nurse.	**Potrzebuję lekarza/pielęgniarki.** _poh·tsheh·boo·yeh leh·kah·zhah/ pyeh·lehng·n'yahr·kee_
When are visiting hours?	**Jakie są godziny odwiedzin?** _yah·kyeh sohm goh·djee·nyh ohd·vyeh·dj'een_
I'm visiting...	**Odwiedzam...** _ohd·vyeh·dzahm..._

YOU MAY HEAR...

Musimy zrobić rentgen. _moo·shee·myh zroh·beech' rehnt·gehn_	We must X-ray you.
Proszę podpisać zgodę na operację. _proh·sheh poht·pee·sahch' zgoh·deh nah oh·peh·rah·tsyeh_	Please sign the consent for surgery.

Dentist

I've lost a filling.	**Wypadła mi plomba.** _vyh·pahd·wah mee plohm·bah_
I've lost a tooth.	**Wypadł mi ząb.** _vyh·pahdw mee zohmp_
I have a toothache.	**Boli mnie ząb.** _boh·lee mn'yeh zohmp_
Can you fix this denture?	**Czy da się naprawić tę protezę?** _chyh dah sh'yeh nah·prah·veech' teh proh·teh·zeh_
I'd like an anesthetic.	**Poproszę znieczulenie.** _poh·proh·sheh zn'yeh·choo·leh·n'yeh_

Gynecologist

I have menstrual cramps/ a vaginal infection.	**Mam bóle miesiączkowe/infekcję pochwy.** *mahm boo·leh myeh·sh'yohn·chkoh·veh/ een·fehk·tsyeh poh·hfyh*
I missed my period.	**Spóźnia mi się okres.** *spoo·zh'n'yah mee sh'yeh ohk·rehs*
I'm on the pill.	**Biorę pigułki antykoncepcyjne.** *byoh·reh pee·goow·kee ahn·tyh·kohn·tsep·tsyhy·neh*
I'm (not) pregnant.	**(Nie) Jestem w ciąży.** *(n'yeh) yehs·tehm fch'yohn·zhyh*
I haven't had my period for...months.	**Nie miałam okresu od...miesięcy.** *n'yeh myah·wahm oh·kreh·soo oht...myeh·sh'yen·tsyh*

For Numbers, see page 171.

Optician

I've lost...	**Zgubiłem m /Zgubiłam f ...** *zgoo·bee·wehm/ zgoo·bee·wahm ...*
a contact lens	**soczewkę kontaktową** *soh·chehf·keh kohn·tahk·toh·vohm*
my glasses	**okulary** *oh·koo·lah·ryh*
a lens	**soczewkę** *soh·chef·keh*

Payment & Insurance

How much?	**Ile to kosztuje?** *ee·leh toh kohsh·too·yeh*
Can I pay by credit card?	**Czy mogę zapłacić kartą kredytową?** *chyh moh·geh zah·pwah·ch'eech' kahr·tohm kreh·dyh·toh·vohm*
I have insurance.	**Mam ubezpieczenie.** *mam oo·behs·pyeh·che·n'yeh*
Can I have a receipt for my insurance?	**Czy mogę dostać pokwitowanie dla mojego ubezpieczenia?** *chyh moh·geh dohs·tach' poh·kfee·toh·vah·n'yeh dlah moh·yeh·goh oo·behs·pyeh·cheh·n'yah*

161

Pharmacy

ESSENTIAL

Where's the nearest (24-hour) pharmacy?
Gdzie jest najbliższa apteka (całodobowa)? *gdj'yeh yest nay‑bleesh‑sha ah‑pteh‑kah (tsah‑woh‑doh‑boh‑vah)*

What time does the pharmacy open/close?
O której otwierają/zamykają aptekę? *oh ktoo‑rey oht‑fyeh‑rah‑yohm/zah‑myh‑kah‑ yohm ah‑pteh‑keh*

What would you recommend for...?
Co może mi pan polecić na...? *tsoh moh‑zheh mee pahn poh‑leh‑ch'eech' nah...*

How much do I take?
Ile mam brać? *ee‑leh mahm brahch'*

Can you fill this prescription?
Czy możecie zrealizować tę receptę? *chyh moh‑zheh‑ch'yeh zreh‑ah‑lee‑zoh‑vach' teh reh‑tsehp‑teh*

I'm allergic to...
Mam uczulenie na... *mahm oo‑choo‑leh‑n'yeh nah...*

Pharmacies in Poland are easily identifiable by the sign **APTEKA** and a cross. Hours are generally from 9:00 a.m. to 6:00 p.m.; some operate around the clock. The names and locations of these 24-hour pharmacies are posted on the doors and windows of other pharmacies. You will need a prescription for drugs not available over the counter. Most pharmacies nowadays sell toiletries and cosmetics, too.

What to Take

I'd like some medicine for…	**Poproszę lekarstwo na…**	poh·_proh_·sheh leh·_kahrs_·tfoh nah…
a cold	**przeziębienie**	psheh·zh'yehm·_byeh_·n'yeh
a cough	**kaszel**	_kah_·shehl
a headache	**ból głowy**	boohl _gwoh_·vyh
diarrhea	**biegunkę**	byeh·_goon_·keh
the flu	**grypę**	_gryh_·peh
motion [travel] sickness	**chorobę lokomocyjną**	hoh·_roh_·beh loh·koh·moh·_tsyhy_·nohm
a sore throat	**ból gardła**	bool _gahr_·dwah
a toothache	**ból zęba**	boohl zehm·bah
an upset stomach	**rozstrój żołądka**	_rohs_·strooy zhoh·_wohnt_·kah
How much should I take?	**Ile mam wziąć?**	_ee_·leh mahm vzh'yonch'
How often should I take it?	**Jak często mam to brać?**	yahk _chehn_·stoh mahm toh brahch'
Is it suitable for children?	**Czy to jest odpowiednie dla dzieci?**	chyh toh yest oht·poh·_vyehd_·n'yeh dlah _dj'yeh_·ch'ee
I'm on…	**Biorę…**	_byoh_·reh…
Are there side effects?	**Czy są jakieś efekty uboczne?**	chyh sohm yah·kyesh' eh·_fehk_·tyh oo·_bohch_·neh

YOU MAY SEE...

RAZ/TRZY RAZY DZIENNIE	once/three times a day
TABLETKA	tablet
KROPLA	drop
ŁYŻECZKA	teaspoon
PRZED POSIŁKIEM	before meals
PO/W TRAKCIE POSIŁKU	after/with meals
NA CZCZO	on an empty stomach
POŁYKAĆ W CAŁOŚCI	swallow whole
MOŻE POWODOWAĆ SENNOŚĆ	may cause drowsiness
WYŁĄCZNIE DO UŻYTKU ZEWNĘTRZNEGO	for external use only

Basic Supplies

I'd like...	**Poproszę...** poh‑_proh_‑sheh...
acetaminophen [paracetamol]	**paracetamol** pah‑rah‑tseh‑_tah_‑mohl
antiseptic cream	**krem aseptyczny** krehm ah‑sehp‑_tyhch_‑nyh
aspirin	**aspirynę** ah‑spee‑_ryh_‑neh
a bandage	**bandaż** _bahn_‑dahzh
a comb	**grzebień** _gzheh_‑byen'
condoms	**prezerwatywy** preh‑zehr‑vah‑_tyh_‑vyh
contact lens solution	**płyn do soczewek kontaktowych** pwyhn doh soh‑_cheh_‑vehk kohn‑tahk‑_toh_‑vyh
deodorant	**dezodorant** deh‑zoh‑_doh_‑rahnt
a hairbrush	**szczotkę do włosów** _shchoht_‑keh doh _vwoh_‑soof
hair spray	**lakier do włosów** _lah_‑kyehr doh _vwoh_‑soof
ibuprofen	**ibuprofen** ee‑boo‑_proh_‑fehn
insect repellent	**środek na owady** _sh'roh_‑dehk nah oh‑_vah_‑dyh
lotion	**balsam** _bahl_‑sahm

a nail file	**pilnik do paznokci** _peel•n'eek doh pahz•nohk•ch'ee_
painkillers	**środki przeciwbólowe** _sh'roht•kee psheh•ch'eef•boo•loh•veh_
a (disposable) razor	**(jednorazową) maszynkę do golenia** _(yehd•noh•rah•zoh•vohm) mah•shyhn•keh doh goh•leh•n'yah_
razor blades	**żyletki** _zhyh•leht•kee_
sanitary napkins [towels]	**podpaski** _poht•pahs•kee_
shampoo/conditioner	**szampon/odżywkę** _shahm•pohn/ohd•zhyhf•keh_
soap	**mydło** _myh•dwoh_
sunscreen	**krem do opalania** _krehm doh oh•pah•lah•n'yah_
tampons	**tampony** _tahm•poh•nyh_
tissues	**chusteczki papierowe** _hoos•tech•kee pahp•yeh•roh•veh_
toilet paper	**papier toaletowy** _pah•pyehr toh•ah•leh•toh•vyh_
a toothbrush	**szczoteczkę do zębów** _shchoh•tech•keh doh zehm•boof_
toothpaste	**pastę do zębów** _pah•steh doh zehm•boof_

For Baby Essentials, see page 148.

The Basics

Grammar

> In Polish, there are two forms for you: **ty** (singular) and **wy** (plural). These are used when talking to relatives, close friends and children as well as among young people. When addressing someone in a formal situation use **pan** (Mr/sir), **pani** (Mrs/Ms/ma'am [madam]) or **państwo** (for groups).

Regular Verbs

Polish verbs are conjugated based on person, number, tense and gender. Following are the present, past and future forms of the verbs **robić** (to do) and **mieć** (to have).

The following abbreviations are used in this section: sing. = singular; pl. = plural; fml. = formal;

ROBIĆ (to do)		Present	Past	Future
I	**ja**	robię	robiłem *m* robiłam *f*	będę robić
you	**ty**	robi**sz**	robiłe**ś** *m* robiła**ś** *f*	będzie**sz** robić
he/sir	**on/ pan**	robi	robił *m*	będzie robić
she/madam	**ona/ pani**	robi	robił**a** *f*	będzie robić
it	**ono**	robi	robił**o**	będzie robić
we	**my**	robi**my**	robi**liśmy** *m* robi**łyśmy** *f*	będzie**my** robić

you	**wy**	robi**cie**	robi**liście** m	będziecie robić
			robi**łyście** f	
they	**oni** m / robi**ą**	robili m	będą robić
	one f /	robi**ły** f	
(pl. fml.)	**państwo**		

MIEĆ (to have)		Present	Past	Future
I	**ja**	mam	mia**łem** m	będę mieć
			mia**łam** f	
you	**ty**	masz	mia**łeś** m	będziesz mieć
			mia**łaś** f	
he/sir	**on/**	ma	miał m	będzie mieć
	pan			
she/madam	**ona/**	ma	mia**ła** f	będzie mieć
	pani			
it	**ono**	ma	miało	będzie mieć
we	**my**	mamy	mieli**śmy** m	będziemy mieć
			mial**yśmy** f	
you	**wy**	macie	mieli**ście** m	będziecie mieć
			miał**yście** f	
they	**oni** m / maj**ą**	mieli m	będą mieć
	one f /	mia**ły** f	
(pl. fml.)	**państwo**		

Irregular Verbs

Irregular verbs are not conjugated by following the normal rules. Following are two common irregular verbs, **być** (to be) and **iść** (to go):

BYĆ (to be)		Present	Past	Future
I	**ja**	jestem	był**em** m	będę
			był**am** f	
you	**ty**	jesteś	był**eś** m	będziesz

			byłaś f	
he/sir	**on/ pan**	jest	był m	będzie
she/madam	**ona/ pani**	jest	była f	będzie
it	**ono**	jest	było	będzie
we	**my**	jesteśmy	byliśmy m byłyśmy f	będziemy
you	**wy**	jesteście	byliście m byłyście f	będziecie
they (pl. fml.)	**oni** m / **one** f / **państwo**	są	byli m były f	będą

IŚĆ (to go)		**Present**	**Past**	**Future**
I	**ja**	idę	szedłem m szłam f	będę iść
you	**ty**	idziesz	szedłeś m szłaś f	będziesz iść
he/sir	**on/ pan**	idzie	szedł m	będzie iść
she/madam	**ona /pani**	idzie	szła f	będzie iść
it	**ono**	idzie	szło	będzie iść
we	**my**	idziemy	szliśmy m szłyśmy f	będziemy iść
you	**wy**	idziecie	szliście m szłyście f	będziecie iść
they (pl. fml.)	**oni** m / **one** f / **państwo**	idą	szli m szły f	będą iść

Nouns

Nouns in Polish are either masculine, feminine or neuter. Masculine nouns usually end in a consonant. Feminine nouns usually end in **–a** or, less often, **–i**. Neuter nouns end in **–ę** or **–o**. Most masculine and feminine nouns, when plural, end in **–y** or in **–i**; most neuter nouns in **–a**.

The endings of nouns vary according to their role in the sentence. There are seven different cases (roles) in both the singular and plural.

There are no articles (a, an, the) in Polish.

Word Order

Word order in Polish is usually as in English, i.e., subject-verb-object. However, word order can be more flexible, because the word endings indicate the role of each word in the sentence.

Example: **Ania dała książkę Markowi.** = **Ania dała Markowi książkę.**
                      = **Ania Markowi dała książkę.** (Ania gave Marek a book.)

To ask a question in Polish:

1. use **czy**

Example: **Czy to pan Kowalski?** Is it Mr. Kowalski?

2. add rising intonation to an affirmative statement

Example: **Pan Kowalski?** Mr. Kowalski?

3. use question words

                      gdzie, kiedy, kto, co where, when, who, what

Example: **Gdzie jesteś?** Where are you?

                      Kiedy wrócisz? When are you coming back?

                      Co będziemy robić? What are we going to do?

Negation

To form a negative sentence, add **nie** (not) before the verb. Note that noun endings may change.

Example: **Mam bilet.** I have a ticket.

Nie mam biletu. I don't have a ticket.

Imperatives

Imperative sentences are formed by adding the appropriate ending to the verb stem.

Example: Go!

you	**ty**	**Idź!**
he/sir	**on/pan**	**Niech idzie!**
she/madam	**ona/pani**	**Niech idzie!**
it	**ono**	**Niech idzie!**
we	**my**	**Idźmy!**
you	**wy**	**Idźcie!**
they (pl. fml.)	**oni** *m* /**one** *f*	**Niech idą!**
		Niech państwo idą!

Adjectives

Adjectives must agree in gender, number and case with the nouns they modify. Masculine adjectives usually end in **–y** or **–i**. The feminine and neuter endings are –a and –e, respectively.

Example: **To duży m dom** *m*. This is a big house.

To duża f szkoła *f*. This is a big school.

To duże dziecko. This is a big child.

Comparative & Superlative

The comparative is usually formed by adding **–szy** *m* /**–sza** *f* /**–sze** *(neuter)* and the superlative by adding **naj...–szy** *m* /**–sza** *f* /**–sze** *(neuter)*.

Example:

tani (cheap)	**tańszy**	**najtańszy**

Less common adjectives often use the complex comparative and superlative form:

comparative = **bardziej** (more) + adjective

superlative = **najbardziej** (the most) + adjective

Example:

tradycyjny (traditional)   **bardziej tradycyjny**   **najbardziej tradycyjny**

Adverbs

Some adverbs in Polish are formed from adjectives by adding the ending **–o**, but there is no fixed rule.

Example: **To szybki samochód.** This is a fast car. (adjective)

Robert jeździ szybko samochodem. Robert drives his car fast. (adverb)

Numbers

ESSENTIAL

0	**zero** *zeh•roh*
1	**jeden** *yeh•dehn*
2	**dwa** *dvah*
3	**trzy** *tshyh*
4	**cztery** *chteh•ryh*
5	**pięć** *pyehn'ch'*
6	**sześć** *shehsh'ch'*
7	**siedem** *sh'yeh•dehm*
8	**osiem** *oh•sh'yehm*
9	**dziewięć** *dj'yeh•vyehn'ch'*
10	**dziesięć** *dj'yeh•sh'yehn'ch'*
11	**jedenaście** *yeh•deh•nahsh'•ch'yeh*
12	**dwanaście** *dvah•nahsh'•ch'yeh*
13	**trzynaście** *tshyh•nahsh'•ch'yeh*

14	**czternaście** *chtehr•nahsh'•ch'yeh*
15	**piętnaście** *pyeht•nahsh'•ch'yeh*
16	**szesnaście** *shehs•nahsh'•ch'yeh*
17	**siedemnaście** *sh'yehdehm•nahsh'•ch'yeh*
18	**osiemnaście** *oh•sh'yehm•nahsh'•ch'yeh*
19	**dziewiętnaście** *dj'yeh•vyeht•nahsh'•ch'yeh*
20	**dwadzieścia** *dvah•dj'yehsh'•ch'yah*
21	**dwadzieścia jeden** *dvah•dj'yehsh'•ch'yah yeh•dehn*
22	**dwadzieścia dwa** *dvah•dj'yehsh'•ch'yah dvah*
30	**trzydzieści** *tshyh•dj'yehsh'•ch'ee*
40	**czterdzieści** *chtehr•dj'yehsh'•ch'ee*
50	**pięćdziesiąt** *pyehn'•dj'yeh•sh'yohnt*
60	**sześćdziesiąt** *shehsh'•dj'yeh•sh'yont*
70	**siedemdziesiąt** *sh'yeh•dehm•dj'yeh•sh'yohnt*
80	**osiemdziesiąt** *oh•sh'yehm•dj'yeh•sh'yohnt*
90	**dziewięćdziesiąt** *dj'eh•vyen'•dj'yeh•sh'ohnt*
100	**sto** *stoh*
101	**sto jeden** *stoh•yeh•dehn*
200	**dwieście** *dvyehsh'•ch'yeh*
500	**pięćset** *pyehnch'•seht*
1,000	**tysiąc** *tyh•sh'yohnts*
10,000	**dziesięć tysięcy** *dj'yeh•sh'yehn'ch' tyh•sh'yen•tsyh*
1,000,000	**milion** *meel•yohn*

Ordinal Numbers

first	**pierwszy** *pyehr•vshyh*
second	**drugi** *droo•gee*
third	**trzeci** *tsheh•ch'ee*
fourth	**czwarty** *chfahr•tyh*
fifth	**piąty** *pyohn•tyh*

once	**raz** *rahs*	
twice	**dwa razy** *dvah rah·zyh*	
three times	**trzy razy** *tshyh rah·zyh*	

In Polish, as in the majority of European countries, a comma is used in place of a decimal point, and gaps are used in long numbers in place of commas. Example: 1 234 567,89 **jeden milion, dwieście trzydzieści cztery tysiące, pięćset sześćdziesiąt siedem, osiemdziesiąt dziewięć.**

Time

ESSENTIAL

What time is it?	**Czy może mi pan powiedzieć, która godzina?** *chyh moh·zheh mee pahn poh·vyeh·dj'yehch' ktoo·rah goh·djee·nah*
five after [past] five	**pięć po piątej** *pyehn'ch' poh pyohn·tehy*
quarter to nine	**za piętnaście dziewiąta** *zah pyeht·nahsh'·ch'yeh dj'yeh·vyohn·tah*
ten to seven	**za dziesięć siódma** *zah dj'yeh·sh'yehn'ch' sh'yood·mah*
5:30 a.m./p.m.	**piąta trzydzieści rano/siedemnasta trzydzieści** *pyohn·tah tshyh·djyehsh'·ch'ee rah·noh/ sh'yeh·dehm·nahs·tah tshyh·djyehsh'·ch'ee*
It's noon [midday].	**Jest południe.** *yehst poh·wood·n'yeh*
It's midnight.	**Jest północ.** *yehst poow·nohts*

In Poland, time is expressed using the 24-hour clock. However, in ordinary conversation, time is usually expressed using numbers 1 to12 with the addition of **rano** (morning), **po południu** (afternoon) or **wieczorem** (evening).

Days

ESSENTIAL

Monday	**poniedziałek**	_poh·n'yeh·dj'yah'·wehk_
Tuesday	**wtorek**	_ftoh·rehk_
Wednesday	**środa**	_sh'roh·dah_
Thursday	**czwartek**	_chfahr·tehk_
Friday	**piątek**	_pyohn·tehk_
Saturday	**sobota**	_soh·boh·tah_
Sunday	**niedziela**	_n'yeh·dj'yeh·lah_

Dates

yesterday	**wczoraj**	_fchoh·rahy_
today	**dzisiaj**	_dj'ee·sh'yahy_
tomorrow	**jutro**	_yoot·roh_
day	**dzień**	_dj'yehn'_
week	**tydzień**	_tyh·dj'yehn'_
month	**miesiąc**	_myeh·sh'ohnts_
year	**rok**	_rohk_

Months

January	**styczeń**	_styh·chehn'_
February	**luty**	_loo·tyh_

March	**marzec** _mah_•zhehts
April	**kwiecień** _kfyeh_•ch'yehn'
May	**maj** _mahy_
June	**czerwiec** _chehr_•vyehts
July	**lipiec** _lee_•pyehts
August	**sierpień** _sh'yehr_•pyehn'
September	**wrzesień** _vzheh_•sh'yehn'
October	**paędziernik** _pahzh'_•_dj'yehr_•n'eek
November	**listopad** _lees_•_toh_•paht
December	**grudzień** _groo_•dj'yehn'

Seasons

spring	**wiosna** _vyohs_•nah
summer	**lato** _lah_•toh
fall [autumn]	**jesień** _yeh_•sh'yehn'
winter	**zima** _zh'ee_•mah

Holidays

January 1	**Nowy Rok** _New Year's Day_
January 6	**Trzech Króli** _Epiphany_
March/April (moveable)	**Wielkanoc** _Easter_
May 1	**Święto 1 Maja** _Labor Day_
May 3	**Konstytucja 3 Maja** _Constitution Day_
Thursday in May/June (moveable)	**Boże Ciało** _Corpus Christi_
August 15	**Wniebowzięcie** _Assumption Day_
November 1	**Wszystkich Świętych** _All Saints' Day_
November 11	**Święto Niepodległości** _Independence Day_
December 25 & 26	**Boże Narodzenie** _Christmas_

Conversion Tables

When you know	Multiply by	To find
ounces	*28.3*	grams
pounds	*0.45*	kilograms
inches	*2.54*	centimeters
feet	*0.3*	meters
miles	*1.61*	kilometers
square inches	*6.45*	sq. centimeters
square feet	*0.09*	sq. meters
square miles	*2.59*	sq. kilometers
pints (U.S./Brit)	*0.47/0.56*	liters
gallons (U.S./Brit)	*3.8/4.5*	liters
Fahrenheit	*5/9, after 32*	Centigrade
Centigrade	*9/5, then +32*	Fahrenheit

Kilometers to Miles Conversions	
1 km	0.62 miles
5 km	3.1 miles
10 km	6.2 miles
50 km	31 miles
100 km	62 miles

Measurement		
1 gram	**gram** *grahm*	= 0.035 oz.
1 kilogram (kg)	**kilo** *kee·loh*	= 2.2 lb
1 liter (l)	**litr** *leetre*	= 1.06 U.S./ 0.88 Brit. quarts
1 centimeter (cm)	**centymetr** *tsehn·tyh·mehtr*	= 0.4 inch
1 meter (m)	**metr** *mehtr*	= 3.28 feet
1 kilometer (km)	**kilometr** *kee·loh·mehtr*	= 0.62 mile

Temperature

-40°C – -40°F	**-1°C** – 30°F	**20°C** – 68°F
-30°C – -22°F	**0°C** – 32°F	**25°C** – 77°F
-20°C – -4°F	**5°C** – 41°F	**30°C** – 86°F
-10°C – 14°F	**10°C** – 50°F	**35°C** – 95°F
-5°C – 23°F	**15°C** – 59°F	

Oven Temperature

100°C – 212°F	**177°C** – 350°F
121°C – 250°F	**204°C** – 400°F
149°C – 300°F	**260°C** – 500°F

A

a little trochę
a lot dużo
a.m. przed południem
accept *v* zaakceptować
accident (road) wypadek
accidentally przypadkowo
across przez
acrylic *adj* akrylowy; *n* akryl
actor aktor
adapter przejściówka
address adres
admission charge opłata za wstęp
adult *n* dorosły
afraid przestraszony
after (time) po; **(place)** za
afternoon popołudnie
aftershave płyn po goleniu
ago temu
agree zgadzać się
air conditioner klimatyzator
air conditioning klimatyzacja
air mattress materac nadmuchiwany

air pump kompresor
airline linia lotnicza
airmail poczta lotnicza
airport lotnisko
air-sickness bag torebka na chorobę lotniczą
aisle seat miejsce przy przejściu
alarm clock budzik
allergic uczulony
allergy uczulenie
allowance ilość
almost prawie
alone sam
already już
also również
alter poprawić
aluminum foil folia aluminiowa
always zawsze
amazing zdumiewający
ambassador ambasador
ambulance karetka
American *adj* amerykański; *n* Amerykanin
amount (money) kwota
and i

| **adj** adjective | **BE** British English | **prep** preposition |
| **adv** adverb | **n** noun | **v** verb |

anesthetia znieczulenie
animal zwierzę
another inny
antacid środek neutralizujący kwas
antibiotics antybiotyk
antique *n* antyk
antiseptic aseptyczny
antiseptic cream krem aseptyczny
any jakiś
anyone ktoś
apartment mieszkanie
apologize przepraszać
appendix wyrostek robaczkowy
appetite apetyt
appetizer przekąska
appointment (business) spotkanie; **(doctor)** wizyta
approximately około
arcade salon gier
area code numer kierunkowy
arm (body part) ramię
around (time) około; **(place)** po
arrive (car, train) przyjeżdżać; **(plane)** lądować
art gallery galeria sztuki
artist artysta
ashtray popielniczka
ask (question) pytać; **(request)** prosić
aspirin aspiryna
asthma astma

at (time) o; **(place)** na
ATM bankomat
attack atak
attractive atrakcyjny
audioguide przewodnik dźwiękowy
Australia Australia
authenticity autentyczność
automatic trasmission automatycza skrzynia biegów
autumn [BE] jesień
available (free) wolne
avalanche lawina

B

baby dziecko
baby food jedzenie dla dzieci
baby wipe wilgotne chusteczki pielęgnacyjne
babysitter opiekunka
back (head) tył; **(body)** grzbiet
backache ból grzbietu
backpack *n* plecak; *v* wędrować z plecakiem
bad zły
bag torba
baggage [BE] bagaż
baggage room przechowalnia bagażu
bakery piekarnia
balcony balkon

ball piłka
ballet balet
band (music) zespół
bandage bandaż
bank bank
bar bar
barber fryzjer męski
basement piwnica
basketball koszykówka
bath *n* wanna; *v* kąpiel
bathroom łazienka
battery bateria; **(car)** akumulator
battle site pole bitwy
be być
beach plaża
beautiful piękny
because ponieważ
bed łóżko
bedding pościel
bedroom sypialnia
before (time) przed
begin zaczynać
beginner początkujący
behind za
belong należeć
belt pasek
berth (ship) koja; **(train)** kuszetka
best najlepszy
better lepszy
between pomiędzy
bib śliniaczek

bicycle rower
bicycle route szlak rowerowy
big duży
bikini bikini
bill (restaurant) rachunek
binoculars lornetka
bird ptak
birthday urodziny
bite *n* ugryzienie
bitter gorzki
bizarre dziwaczny
black czarny
bladder pęcherz moczowy
bland mdły
blanket koc
bleach wybielacz
bleed krwawić
bleeding krwotok
blister pęcherz
block *v* blokować
blood krew
blood pressure ciśnienie krwi
blouse bluzka
blow-dry suszenie z modelowaniem
blue niebieski
board pokład
boarding card karta pokładowa
boat trip przejażdżka statkiem
boil *v* gotować
boiler boiler

bone kość
book książka
bookstore księgarnia
boots botki
boring nudny
born v urodzić się
borrow pożyczyć
botanical garden ogród botaniczny
bottle butelka
bottle opener otwieracz do butelek
bowl miska
box (container) pudełko
boy chłopiec
boyfriend chłopak
bra biustonosz
bracelet bransoletka
brake hamulec
break (destroy) zepsuć; **(body part)** złamać
break down (go wrong) zepsuć się
breakfast śniadanie
breast (body) pierś
breathe oddychać
bridge most
briefs (clothing) majtki
bring przenieść
Britain Wielka Brytania
British adj brytyjski; n Brytyjczyk
brochure broszura

broken zepsuty
bronchitis bronchit
brooch broszka
brother brat
browse patrzeć
bruise siniak
bucket wiaderko
bug robak
build budować
building budynek
bulletin board tablica informacyjna
burn n oparzenie
bus autobus
bus route trasa autobusowa
bus station dworzec autobusowy
bus stop przystanek autobusowy
business biznes
business class klasa biznes
busy zajęty
but ale
butane gas butan
butcher (store) rzeźnik
button guzik
buy kupić

C

cabaret kabaret
café kawiarnia
call (ambulance) wezwać; **(telephone)** zadzwonić

camera aparat fotograficzny
camera case futerał na aparat
camp *n* obóz; *v* obozować
campfire ognisko
campsite pole namiotowe
can *n* puszka; *v* móc
can opener otwieracz do puszek
Canada Kanada
canal kanał
cancel odwołać
cancer rak
cap (dental) koronka; **(clothing)** czapka
car samochód; **(train)** wagon
car hire [BE] wynajem samochodów
car insurance ubezpiecznie samochodowe
car park parking
car rental wynajem samochodów
car seat fotelik dziecięcy
carafe karafka
card karta
careful ostrożny
carpet dywan
carry-on (luggage) bagaż podręczny
cart wózek
carton karton
cash (money) gotówka; *v* zrealizować

cashier kasjer
casino kasyno
castle zamek
catch (bus) złapać
cathedral katedra
cave jaskinia
CD płyta
CD player odtwarzacz płyt kompaktowych
cell phone telefon komórkowy
cemetery cmentarz
ceramics ceramika
certificate certyfikat
chain łańcuszek
change *n* **(small coins)** drobne; **(in shop)** reszta; *v* **(bus, train)** przesiadać się; **(baby)** przewinąć; **(money)** wymieniać; **(reservation)** zmienić, **(clothes)** przebrać się
changing room przebieralnia
charcoal węgiel drzewny
charge opłata
cheap tani
check *n* czek
check in *n* odprawa
check out (hotel) wyrejestrować się
checkbook książeczka czekowa
check-in desk stanowisko odprawy

chemical toilet chemiczna toaleta
chemist [BE] apteka
cheque [BE] czek
chess szachy
chest (body) klatka persiowa
child dziecko
child's cot łóżeczko dziecięce
child's seat krzesełko dla dziecka
church kościół
cigar cygaro
cigarette papieros
clamp założyć blokadę na koła
clean adj czysty; v wyczyścić
cliff klif
cling film [BE] folia do żywności
clinic klinika
clock zegar
close (near) niedaleko; **(store)** zamykać
clothing store sklep odzieżowy
cloudy pochmurno
coach [BE] (long-distance bus) autokar
coat płaszcz
coat check szatnia
coat hanger wieszak
cockroach karaluch
coin moneta
cold adj zimny; adv zimno; n **(illness)** przeziębienie

collapse upaść
collect zebrać
collect call rozmowa na koszt rozmówcy
color kolor
color film film kolorowy
comb grzebień
come przyjść
come back (return) wrócić
commission prowizja
company (companionship) towarzystwo; **(business)** firma
compartment (train) przedział
composer kompozytor
computer komputer
concert koncert
concert hall sala koncertowa
concession koncesja
concussion wstrząs mózgu
conditioner odżywka
condom prezerwatywa
conductor dyrygent
confirm potwierdzić
confirmation potwierdzenie
connect (internet) połączyć się z siecią
connection (train) połączenie
conscious (awake) przytomny
constant ciągły
constipation zaparcie
consulate konsulat

consult skonsultować się
contact skontaktować się
contact lens szkło kontaktowe
contagious zakaźny
contain zawierać
contraceptive środek antykoncepcyjny
convenience store sklep osiedlowy
cook v gotować; n kucharz
cooker [BE] kuchenka
cooking (cuisine) kuchnia
cooking facilities możliwość gotowania
copper miedź
copy kopia
corkscrew korkociąg
correct prawidłowy
cosmetics kosmetyki
cost v kosztować
cot rozkładane łóżko
cottage domek
cotton (material) bawełna
cough n kaszel; v kaszleć
country kraj
country code numer kierunkowy
country music muzyka country
course (meal) danie; **(path)** droga
cousin kuzyn
cramp skurcz
credit card karta kredytowa

credit card number numer karty kredytowej
crib łóżeczko dziecięce
cross v przejść
cross-country skis biegówki
crowd tłok
crowded zatłoczony
crown (dental) koronka; **(royal)** korona
cruise n rejs
crystal (quartz) kryształ
cup filiżanka
cupboard szafka kuchenna
currency waluta
currency exchange office kantor
currency exchange rate kurs wymiany
curtain zasłona
customs urząd celny
customs declaration deklaracja celna
cut (hair) strzyżenie; **(wound)** rana cięta
cut glass cięte szkło
cutlery sztućce
cycling kolarstwo

D

daily adj codzienny; adv codziennie
damaged zniszczony

damp *adj* wilgotny
dance *n* taniec; *v* tańczyć
dance club dyskoteka
dangerous niebezpieczny
dark ciemny
daughter córka
dawn świt
day dzień
day charge opłata za dzień
day ticket bilet jednodniowy
day trip wycieczka jednodniowa
dead (battery) wyczerpany
deaf głuchy
deck chair leżak
declare zadeklarować
deduct odejmować
deep głęboki
defrost rozmrozić
degree (temperature) stopień
delay opóźnienie
delayed opóźniony
delicatessen delikatesy
delicious smaczny
deliver dostarczyć
delivery dostawa
denim drelich
dental floss nić dentystyczna
dentist dentysta
denture proteza dentystyczna
deodorant dezodorant
depart (train, bus) odjeżdżać;

(plane) startować
department store dom towarowy
departure lounge poczekalnia
departures (airport) hala odlotów
deposit (security) kaucja
describe opisać
description opis
destination (travel) cel podróży
detail szczegół
detergent środek czystości
develop (photos) wywołać
diabetes cukrzyca
diabetic *n* cukrzyk
dialing code numer kierunkowy
diamond brylant
diaper pieluszka
diarrhea biegunka
dice kostka do gry
dictionary słownik
diesel diesel
diet dieta
difficult trudny
dining car wagon restauracyjny
dining room jadalnia
dinner kolacja
direct *adj* **(train, journey)**
  bezpośredni; *v* **(to a place)**
  wskazać kierunek
direction kierunek
director (company) dyrektor
directory (telephone) książka

telefoniczna
dirty brudny
disabled *n* niepełnosprawny
discount zniżka
discount card karta rabatowa
dish (meal) danie
dishcloth ścierka
dishwasher zmywarka
dishwashing liquid płyn do
zmywania
display cabinet gablota
display case gablota
disposable camera aparat
jednorazowy
disturb przeszkadzać
dive (scuba dive) nurkować; **(jump)**
skakać
diving equipment sprzęt do
nurkowania
divorced rozwiedziony
dizziness zawroty głowy
do robić
doctor lekarz
doll lalka
dollar dolar
domestic (flight) krajowy
door drzwi
double bed podwójne łóżko
double room pokój dwuosobowy
downtown area centrum
dozen tuzin

dress sukienka
drink *n* **(alcoholic)** drink; *v* pić
drink menu lista drinków
drip ciec
drive jechać
driver (car) kierowca
driver's license prawo jazdy
drown tonąć
drugstore drogeria
drunk pijany
dry cleaner's pralnia chemiczna
dry-clean czyścić **(chemicznie)**
dubbed dubbingowany
dummy [BE] smoczek
during podczas
dustbin [BE] śmietnik
duty cło
duvet kołdra

E

ear ucho
ear drops krople do uszu
earache ból ucha
early *adj* wczesny; *adv* wcześnie
earring kolczyk
east wschód
easy łatwy
eat jeść
economy class klasa turystyczna
elastic *adj* elastyczny
electric shaver golarka elektryczna

electrical outlet gniazdko elektryczne
electronic elektroniczny
elevator winda
e-mail *n* e-mail; *v* napisać maila
e-mail address adres e-mail
embassy ambasada
embroidery haft
emerald szmaragd
emergency nagły wypadek
emergency exit wyjście awaryjne
emergency ward izba przyjęć
empty pusty
enamel emalia
end *n* koniec; *v* kończyć (się)
engaged zaręczony
engine silnik
engineer inżynier
England Anglia
English *adj* angielski; *n* Anglik
enjoy podobać się
enjoyable przyjemny
enlarge (photos) powiększyć
enough dość
entertainment guide program rozrywek
entrance fee opłata za wstęp
envelope koperta
epilepsy epilepsja
epileptic *n* epileptyk
equipment (sports) sprzęt

era epoka
error błąd
escalator schody ruchome
escape route droga ewakuacyjna
essential niezbędny
e-ticket bilet elektroniczny
eurocheque euroczek
European Union Unia Europejska
evening wieczór
evening dress strój wieczorowy
every każdy
examination (medical) badanie
example przykład
except oprócz
excess baggage nadbagaż
exchange wymienić
exchange rate kurs wymiany
excursion wycieczka
exhausted wyczerpany
exit wyjście
expensive drogi
experienced zaawansowany
expiration date data ważności
expiry date [BE] data ważności
exposure (photos) naświetlanie
express ekspres
express mail priorytet
extension (phone) wewnętrzny
extra (additional) dodatkowy
extract (tooth) wyrwać
eye oko

F

fabric materiał
face twarz
facial zabieg oczyszczania skóry
faint v zemdleć
fairground wesołe miasteczko
fall n jesień
family rodzina
famous sławny
fan (electric) wentylator
far daleko
farm gospodarstwo
far-sighted dalekowidz
fast szybko
father ojciec
faucet kran
faulty wadliwy
favorite ulubiony
fax faks
fee opłata
feed nakarmić
feel czuć (się)
female kobieta
ferry prom
fever gorączka
few parę
fiancé narzeczony
fiancée narzeczona
field pole
fight (brawl) bójka
fill out (a form) wypełnić

fill up (car) nalać do pełna
filling (dental) plomba
film (camera, movie) film
filter filtr
find znaleźć
fine (well) dobrze; **(penalty)** grzywna
finger palec
fire pożar
fire alarm alarm pożarowy
fire brigade [BE] straż pożarna
fire department straż pożarna
fire door drzwi przeciwpożarowe
fire escape schody pożarowe
fire exit wyjście awaryjne
fire extinguisher gaśnica
first class pierwsza klasa
first floor parter
fish store sklep rybny
fit v pasować
fitting room przymierzalnia
fix v naprawić
flame płomień
flashlight latarka
flat (tire) przebity
flavor smak
flea pchła
flea market pchli targ
flight lot
flight number numer lotu
floor (level) piętro

florist kwiaciarnia
flower kwiat
flu grypa
flush (toilet) spuszczać wodę
fly *n* mucha; *v* latać
fog mgła
folk art sztuka ludowa
folk music muzyka ludowa
follow (pursue) podążać; **(road, sign)** jechać zgodnie z
food jedzenie
food poisoning zatrucie pokarmowe
foot stopa
football [BE] piłka nożna
footpath [BE] dróżka
for (time) przez; **(duration)** na
foreign currency obca waluta
forest las
forget zapominać
fork widelec
form formularz
formal dress strój formalny
fortunately na szczęście
fountain fontanna
foyer (hotel, theater) foyer
fracture złamanie
frame (glasses) oprawka
free (available) wolny; **(without charge)** bezpłatny
freezer zamrażarka
frequently często

fresh świeży
friend przyjaciel
friendly (person) przyjazny; **(place, atmosphere)** przyjemny
frightened przerażony
from (place) z; **(time)** od
front przód
frost mróz
frying pan patelnia
fuel paliwo
full pełny
full board z pełnym wyżywieniem
fun zabawa
funny śmieszny
furniture meble

G

gallon galon
game gra; **(sports)** mecz
garage (mechanic) warsztat samochodowy; **(parking lot)** garaż
garbage śmieci
garbage bag worek na śmieci
garden ogródek
gas (fuel) benzyna
gas station stacja benzynowa
gate (airport) wyjście
gauze gaza
genuine prawdziwy
get (buy) kupić; **(find)** znaleźć
get back (return) wrócić

get off (bus/train) wysiąść
get to dojechać do
gift prezent
gift shop sklep z upominkami
giftwrap zapakować na prezent
girl dziewczyna
girlfriend dziewczyna
give dać
glass (non-alcoholic) szklanka;
  (alcoholic) kieliszek
glasses (optical) okulary
glove rękawiczka
go (on foot) iść; **(by bus, train)**
  jechać; **(by plane)** lecieć
go away odejść
goggles (swimming) okularki;
  (skiing) gogle
gold złoto
golf golf
golf club kij golfowy
golf course pole golfowe
good dobry
good evening dobry wieczór
good morning dzień dobry
good night dobranoc
goodbye do widzenia
gram gram
grandfather dziadek
grandmother babcia
grandparents dziadkowie
grass trawa

gray szary
great *adj* świetny; *adv* świetnie
green zielony
greengrocer [BE] warzywniak
grocery store sklep spożywczy
ground (earth) ziemia
ground floor [BE] parter
groundcloth podłoga namiotu
groundsheet [BE] podłoga
  namiotu
group grupa
group guide przewodnik grupowy
group leader kierownik grupy
group ticket bilet grupowy
guarantee gwarancja
guest gość
guesthouse pensjonat
guide (tour) przewodnik
guidebook przewodnik
guided tour wycieczka z
  przewodnikiem
guided walk wycieczka piesza z
  przewodnikiem
guitar gitara
gym siłownia
gynecologist ginekolog

H

hair włosy
hair gel żel do włosów
haircut strzyżenie włosów

hairdresser fryzjer
hairspray lakier do włosów
half pół
hammer młotek
hand ręka
hand luggage [BE] bagaż podręczny
hand washable prać ręcznie
handbag torebka
handicapped niepełnosprawny
handicrafts wyroby rękodzielnicze
handkerchief chusteczka
hanger wieszak
hangover n kac
happy szczęśliwy
harbor port
hard (texture) twardy; **(difficult)** ciężki
hat kapelusz
have mieć
hay fever katar sienny
head n głowa; v **(go towards)** jechać w kierunku
head waiter kierownik sali
headache ból głowy
health zdrowie
health food store sklep ze zdrową żywnością
health insurance ubezpieczenie zdrowotne
hear słyszeć

hearing aid aparat słuchowy
heart serce; **(cards)** kier
heart attack zawał serca
heat ogrzewanie
heater grzejnik
heating [BE] ogrzewanie
heavy ciężki
height wzrost
helmet kask
help pomoc
hemorrhoids hemoroidy
her jej
here tutaj
hernia przepuklina
herpes opryszczka
hers jej
high wysoki
highchair wysokie krzesełko
highlight v **(hair)** robić pasemka; **(stress)** podkreślić
highway autostrada
hiking (general) turystyka piesza; **(trip)** wędrówka
hill wzgórze
him niego
hire [BE] v wynająć
his jego
historic site miejsce historyczne
hobby (pastime) hobby
holiday [BE] wakacje
holiday resort miejscowość

wypoczynkowa
home (be/go) w domu/do domu
honeymoon miesiąc miodowy
horse koń
horse racing wyścigi konne
hospital szpital
hot gorący
hot spring gorące źródło
hotel hotel
hour godzina
house dom
housewife gospodyni domowa
hundred sto
hungry głodny
hurt boleć
husband mąż

I

ice-cream parlor lodziarnia
icy oblodzony
identification dowód tożsamości
ill chory
illegal nielegalny
imitation imitacja
in (place) w; **(period of time)** w ciągu
included wliczony
incredible niewiarygodny
indicate wskazywać
indigestion niestrawność
indoor pool kryty basen

inexpensive niedrogi
infected zakażony
infection infekcja
inflammation zapalenie
informal (dress) nieformalny
information (desk, office) infomacja
injection zastrzyk
injured ranny
innocent niewinny
insect insekt
insect bite ugryzienie owada
insect repellent środek na owady
insect sting użądlenie
inside w środku
insist nalegać
insomnia bezsenność
instead zamiast
instruction instrukcja
instructor instruktor
insulin insulina
insurance ubezpieczenie
insurance card polisa ubezpieczeniowa
insurance certificate [BE] polisa ubezpieczeniowa
insurance claim wniosek o odszkodowanie
interest (hobby) zainteresowanie
interested zainteresowany
interesting interesujący

international (flight) międzynarodowy
International Student Card Międzynarodowa Karta Studenta
internet internet
internet cafe kafejka internetowa
interpreter tłumacz ustny
intersection skrzyżowanie
into do
intolerance nietolerancja
invite zaprosić
iodine jodyna
Ireland Irlandia
iron *n* żelazko; *v* prasować
itch swędzieć
item (object) przedmiot
itemized bill szczegółowy rachunek

J

jacket (men's) marynarka; **(women's)** żakiet
jaw szczęka
jazz jazz
jeans dżinsy
jellyfish meduza
jet-ski skuter wodny
jeweler jubiler
jewelry biżuteria
join (a group) dołączyć się
joint (body) staw

joke żart
journalist dziennikarz
journey podróż
jug (water) dzbanek
jumper [BE] pulower
junction [BE] (intersection) skrzyżowanie

K

keep zatrzymać
kerosene nafta
kettle czajnik
key klucz
key card (hotel) karta
kiddie pool brodzik
kidney nerka
kilometer kilometr
kind *adj* uprzejmy; *n* rodzaj
kiss *n* pocałunek; *v* całować
kitchen kuchnia
kitchen foil [BE] folia aluminiowa
knee kolano
knickers [BE] majtki
knife nóż
know wiedzieć
kosher koszerny

L

label (sticker) nalepka; **(on bottle)** etykieta
lace koronka

ladder drabina
lake jezioro
lamp lampa
land *v* lądować
language course kurs językowy
large (size) duży
last *adj* ostatni; **(previous)** zeszły; *v* trwać
late (not early) późny; **(delayed)** opóźniony
later później
laundromat pralnia samoobsługowa
laundry facilitles pralnia
lawyer prawnik
laxative środek przeczyszczający
lead *n* smycz; *v* prowadzić
leader (ideological) przywódca; **(manager)** menedżer
leak *n* przeciek; *v* **(roof, pipe)** przeciekać
learn (language) uczyć się
leather skóra
leave (depart) odjeżdżać; **(deposit)** zostawić; **(on foot)** odejść; **(depart of plane)** odlatywać
left *adj* lewy
left-luggage office [BE] przechowalnia bagażu
leg noga

legal legalny
lend pożyczyć
lens (optical) soczewka; **(camera)** obiektyw
lense cap nakładka na obiektyw
less mniej
lesson lekcja
let *v* **(permit)** pozwolić
let go puścić
letter list
library biblioteka
license plate number numer rejestracyjny
life preserver koło ratunkowe
lifeboat łódź ratunkowa
lifeguard ratownik
lifejacket kamizelka ratunkowa
lift [BE] winda
lift pass (skiing) skipass
light *adj* **(weight)** lekki; **(color)** jasny; *n* światło
light bulb żarówka
lighter *adj* jaśniejszy; *n* zapalniczka
like *v* lubić
limousine limuzyna
line (metro) linia metra
linen len
lip warga
lipgloss błyszczyk
lipstick szminka

liquor store sklep monopolowy
liter litr
little (small) mały
live mieszkać
liver wątroba
living room salon
lobby (theater) foyer; **(hotel)** hol
local lokalny
lock *n* **(door)** zamek; **(bike)** blokada; *v* zamknąć
log off wylogować się
log on zalogować się
login login
long długi
long-distance bus autokar
long-sighted [BE] dalekowidz
loose luźny
lorry [BE] ciężarówka
lose (item) zgubić; **(person)** stracić
lost-and-found biuro rzeczy znalezionych
lost-property office [BE] biuro rzeczy znalezionych
love *n* miłość; *v* kochać
lovely śliczny
low niski
lower (berth) dolny
low-fat o niskiej zawartości tłuszczu
luck szczęście

luggage bagaż
luggage cart wózek na bagaż
luggage locker schowek na bagaż
luggage trolley [BE] wózek na bagaż
lump guz
lunch obiad
lung płuco

M

machine washable prać w pralce
madam pani
magazine czasopismo
magnificent wspaniały
maid pokojówka
mail *n* poczta; *v* wysłać
mailbox skrzynka pocztowa
main główny
make zrobić
male mężczyzna
mallet młotek drewniany
manager menadżer
manicure manicure
many dużo
map mapa
market (job market) rynek; **(place to buy)** targ
married żonaty
mascara tusz do rzęs
mask (diving) maska
mass msza

massage masaż
match (game) mecz; **(light)** zapałka
mattress materac
maybe może
me ja
meal posiłek
measles odra
measure zmierzyć
measurement miara
measuring cup miarka kuchenna
measuring spoon łyżka do odmierzania
mechanic mechanik
medication lek
medicine lekarstwo
medium średni
meet (get to know) poznać; **(appointment)** spotkać
meeting place miejsce zbiórki
meeting point [BE] miejsce zbiórki
member (association) członek
memorial (war) pomnik
mention wspominać
menu menu
message wiadomość
metal metal
metro map mapa metra
metro station stacja metra
microwave (oven) kuchenka mikrofalowa
midday [BE] południe
midnight północ
migraine migrena
million milion
mine mój
mini-bar mini-bar
minute (time) minuta
mirror lustro
miss (lack) brakować; **(lost)** zaginąć
mistake błąd
misunderstanding nieporozumienie
mobile home przyczepa mieszkalna
mobile phone [BE] telefon komórkowy
moisturizer (cream) krem nawilżający
monastery klasztor
money pieniądze
money order przekaz pieniężny
month miesiąc
monument pomnik
mop mop
moped motorower
more więcej
morning rano
mosque meczet
mosquito bite ukąszenie komara

mother matka
motion sickness choroba
 lokomocyjna
motorbike motor
motorboat motorówka
motorcycle motor
motorway [BE] autostrada
mountain góra
mountain bike rower górski
mountain pass przełęcz górska
mountain range łańcuch górski
moustache wąsy
mouth usta
move ruszać
movie film
movie theater kino
much dużo
mug n kubek; v napadać
mugging napad
mumps świnka
muscle mięsień
museum muzeum
music muzyka
music store sklep muzyczny
musician muzyk
must v musieć
my mój

N

name imię
napkin serwetka

nappy [BE] pieluszka
narrow wąski
national narodowy
national park park narodowy
nationality obywatelstwo
native tutejszy
nature reserve rezerwat przyrody
nature trail szlak przyrodniczy
nausea mdłości
near niedaleko
nearby niedaleko
near-sighted krótkowidz
necessary konieczny
neck (body) szyja
necklace naszyjnik
need v potrzebować
nerve nerw
nervous system układ nerwowy
never nigdy
new nowy
newsagent [BE] kiosk z gazetami
newspaper gazeta
newsstand kiosk z gazetami
next następny
nice miły
night noc
night club klub nocny
no nie
noisy hałaśliwy
none żaden
nonsense bzdura

non-smoking *adj* dla niepalących
noon południe
normal normalny
north północ
nose nos
nothing nic
notify zawiadomić
now teraz
number numer
nurse pielęgniarka
nylon nylon

O

occasionally czasami
occupied zajęty
office (place) biuro
off-licence [BE] sklep
  monopolowy
often często
okay okay
old stary
old town stare miasto
on (day, date) w
once raz
one jeden
one-way w jedną stonę
one-way ticket bilet w jedną
  stronę
open *adj* otwarty; *v* otwierać
opening hours godziny otwarcia
opera opera

opera house opera
operation operacja
opposite naprzeciwko
optician optyk
or albo
orange (color) pomarańczowy
order *n* zamówienie; *v* zamówić
our(s) nasz
outdoor pool basen otwarty
outrageous (price) horrendalny
outside na zewnątrz
oval owalny
oven piekarnik
overcharge *v* policzyć za dużo
overheat przegrzać się
overnight na noc
owe być dłużnym
own *adj* własny
owner właściciel

P

p.m. po południu
pacifier smoczek
pack pakować
package przesyłka
paddling pool [BE] brodzik
padlock kłódka
pail (toy) wiaderko
pain ból
painkiller środek przeciwbólowy
paint *v* malować

painter malarz
painting obraz
pair para
palace pałac
panorama panorama
pants spodnie
pantyhose rajstopy
paper napkin serwetka papierowa
paper towel ręcznik papierowy
paracetamol [BE] paracetamol
paralysis paraliż
parcel [BE] paczka
parent rodzic
park *n* park; *v* parkować
parking garage parking podziemny
parking lot parking
parking meter parkometr
parliament building budynek parlamentu
partner partner
party (social) przyjęcie
passenger pasażer
passport paszport
passport number numer paszportu
password hasło
pastry shop sklep cukierniczy
patch załatać
patient *n* pacjent
pavement [BE] chodnik

pay płacić
pay phone automat telefoniczny
payment zapłata
peak szczyt
pearl perła
pedestrian pieszy
pedestrian crossing przejście dla pieszych
pedestrian zone strefa zamknięta dla ruchu kołowego
peg [BE] spinacz do bielizny
pen długopis
per za
perhaps być może
period (time) okres; **(menstrual)** miesiączka
person osoba
petrol [BE] benzyna
petrol station [BE] stacja benzynowa
pewter cyna
pharmacy apteka
phone *n* telefon; *v* dzwonić
phone card karta telefoniczna
photo zdjęcie
photocopier kopiarka
photograph zdjęcie
photographer fotograf
phrase zwrot
phrase book rozmówki
pick up odebrać

picnic piknik

picnic area miejsce piknikowe

piece (item) sztuka; **(amount)** kawałek

pill (contraceptive) pigułka antykoncepcyjna; **(tablet)** tabletka

pillow poduszka

pillow case poszewka na poduszkę

pink różowy

pipe (smoking) fajka

pitch (camping) pole namiotowe

pizzeria pizzeria

place miejsce

plan *n* plan; *v* planować

plane samolot

plant (greenery) roślina

plaster [BE] plaster

plastic *adj* plastikowy

plastic bag torebka plastikowa

plastic wrap folia spożywcza

plate talerz

platform peron; **[BE]** tor

platinum platyna

play *n* **(theater)** sztuka; *v* grać

playground plac zabaw

playing field boisko

pleasant przyjemny

please proszę

plug zatyczka

plunger przepychacz

pneumonia zapalenie płuc

point wskazać

poison trucizna

Poland Polska

police policja

police report raport policyjny

police station komisariat policji

Polish *adj* polski; *n* Polak

pollen count stężenie pyłków w powietrzu

polyester poliester

pond staw

pop (music) pop

popular popularny; **(well-known)** znany

port (harbor) port

porter bagażowy

portion porcja

possible możliwy

post [BE] *n* **(mail)** poczta; *v* wysłać

post office poczta

postage opłata

postcard pocztówka

poster plakat

pot (for cooking) garnek; **(for tea)** dzbanek

pottery ceramika

pound (sterling) funt

powdery (snow) puszysty

power (electricity) prąd

precipice przepaść

pregnant w ciąży
prescribe przepisać
prescription recepta
present (gift) prezent
press naciskać
pretty ładny
price cena
print *n* sztych; *v* drukować
prison więzienie
produce store sklep spożywczy
profession zawód
program program
pronounce wymawiać
pub pub
public *n* publiczność; *adj* publiczny
pump (gas station) pompa
puncture przebicie
pure czysty
purple fioletowy
purse torebka
push-chair [BE] wózek spacerowy
put włożyć

Q

quality jakość
quarter ćwierć; **(time)** kwadrans
queue [BE] *n* kolejka; *v* stać w kolejce
quick szybki
quickly szybko
quiet cichy

R

race course [BE] tor wyścigowy
racetrack tor wyścigowy
racket (tennis, squash) rakieta
railway station [BE] stacja kolejowa
rain *n* deszcz
raincoat płaszcz przeciwdeszczowy
rape *n* gwałt; *v* zgwałcić
rapids progi rzeczne
rare (unusual) rzadki
rash wysypka
razor maszynka do golenia
razor blade żyletka
read *v* czytać
ready gotowy
real (genuine) prawdziwy
rear tylny
receipt paragon
receive odebrać
reception (desk) recepcja
receptionist recepcjonista
recommend polecić
red czerwony
reduction (price) obniżka
refrigerator lodówka
refund zwrot pieniędzy
region (area) region
registered mail list polecony
registration form formularz rejestracji
reliable niezawodny

religion religia
remember pamiętać
rent wynająć
rental car wynajęty samochód
repair *n* naprawa; *v* naprawić
repeat powtórzyć
replacement wymiana
replacement part część zamienna
report (crime) zgłosić
require wymagać
reservation rezerwacja
reservations desk okienko
  rezerwacji
reserve *v* rezerwować
rest *v* odpoczywać
restaurant restauracja
restroom toaleta
return wrócić; **(surrender)** zwrócić
return ticket [BE] bilet powrotny
reverse-charge call [BE] rozmowa
  na koszt rozmówcy
rheumatism reumatyzm
rib żebro
right (correct) poprawny; **(good)**
  dobry
right of way pierwszeństwo
  przejazdu
ring pierścionek
river rzeka
road droga
road map mapa drogowa

road sign znak drogowy
rob obrabować
robbery rabunek
rock (music) rock; **(land
  formation)** skała
romantic romantyczny
roof dach
roof-rack bagażnik dachowy
room (hotel) pokój
room service room service
rope lina
round okrągły
round-trip ticket bilet powrotny
route trasa
rubbish [BE] śmieci
rude niegrzeczny
ruins ruiny

S

safe *adj* bezpieczny; *n* sejf
safety bezpieczeństwo
safety pin agrafka
sand piasek
sandal sandał
sanitary napkin podpaska
sanitary pad [BE] podpaska
satellite TV telewizja satelitarna
satin satyna
saucepan rondel
sauna sauna
say *v* powiedzieć

scarf szalik
scissors nożyczki
Scotland Szkocja
screwdriver śrubokręt
sea morze
seasickness choroba moska
season ticket bilet okresowy
seat (train) miejsce
seat reservation (train) miejscówka
second class druga klasa
secondhand store sklep z używaną odzieżą
secretary sekretarka
sedative środek uspokajający
see (spot) zobaczyć; **(inspect)** sprawdzić; **(observe, witness)** widzieć
self-employed samozatrudniony
self-service (gas station) samoobsługa
sell sprzedawać
send wysłać
senior citizen emeryt
separated w separacji
separately osobno
serious poważny
service (in restaurant) obsługa; **(religious)** nabożeństwo
sex seks; **(gender)** płeć
shade odcień

shady cienisty
shallow płytki
shampoo szampon
share v dzielić
sharp ostry
shaving cream krem do golenia
she ona
sheet (bed) prześcieradło
shirt (men's) koszula; **(women's)** bluzka
shock (electric) porażenie
shoe but
shoe repair naprawa obuwia
shoe store sklep z obuwiem
shop assistant sprzedawca
shopping area centrum handlowe
shopping basket koszyk
shopping cart wózek
shopping centre [BE] centrum handlowe
shopping mall centrum handlowe
shopping trolley [BE] wózek
short adj **(length)** krótki; **(person)** niski
shorts (clothing) szorty
short-sighted [BE] krótkowidz
shoulder bark
shovel (toy) łopatka
show n **(presentation)** pokaz; **(theater)** sztuka; v pokazać
shower prysznic

shrine kapliczka

shut v zamykać; adj zamknięty

shutter okiennica

side (head) bok

side order dodatek

side street boczna uliczka

sidewalk chodnik

sights atrakcje turystyczne

sightseeing tour wycieczka po mieście

sign znak

silk jedwab

silver srebro

singer pieśniarz

single sam

single room pokój jednoosobowy

single ticket bilet w jedną stronę

sink zlew

sir pan

sister siostra

sit siadać

size rozmiar

skate łyżwa

skewer rożen

ski narta

ski boot but narciarski

ski pole kijek

skin skóra

skirt spódnica

sleep spać

sleeper car [BE] wagon sypialny

sleeping bag śpiwór

sleeping car wagon sypialny

sleeping pill tabletka nasenna

sleeve rękaw

slice plasterek

slip v poślizgnąć się

slipper pantofel

slow wolny

slowly wolno

small mały

smell pachnieć

smoke palić

smoking (area) dla palących

snack przekąska

snack bar bar

sneaker tenisówka

snorkel fajka do nurkowania

snow śnieg

soap mydło

soccer piłka nożna

sock skarpetka

socket gniazdko

sole (shoes) podeszwa

some jakiś

something coś

sometimes czasami

somewhere gdzieś

son syn

soon niedługo

sore throat ból gardła

sorry przepraszam

soul (music) soul

sour kwaśne

south południe

souvenir pamiątka

souvenir store sklep z pamiątkami

spa spa

space miejsce

spare zapasowy

speak mówić

special specjalny

specialist specjalista

specimen próbka

spell v przeliterować

spend (time) spędzać; (money) wydawać

spicy ostry

sponge gąbka

spoon łyżka

sport sport

sporting goods store sklep sportowy

spot (place, site) miejsce

sprained skręcony

spring wiosna

square kwadrat

stadium stadion

staff personel

stain plama

stainless steel stal nierdzewna

stairs schody

stamp (postal) znaczek

standby ticket tani bilet okazyjny

start v (begin) zaczynać się; (car) zapalić

starter [BE] przekąska

statement (police) zeznanie

stationery store sklep papierniczy

statue pomnik

stay n pobyt; v zostać; (in a hotel) zatrzymać się

sterilizing solution płyn do sterylizacji

still adv wciąż

stockings [BE] pończochy

stolen ukradziony

stomach brzuch

stomachache ból brzucha

stop n (bus, tram) przystanek; v zatrzymywać się

store sklep

store guide tablica informacyjna

storm burza

stove kuchenka

strange dziwny

straw (drinking) słomka

stream strumień

strong (powerful) silny

student student

study v studiować

style styl

subtitled z napisami
suggest zasugerować
suit (men's) garnitur; **(women's)** kostium
suitable stosowny
suitcase walizka
summer lato
sunbathe opalać się
sunburn oparzenie słoneczne
sunglasses okulary słoneczne
sunny słoneczny
sunshade parasol
sunstroke udar słoneczny
suntan lotion krem do opalania
superb znakomity
supermarket supermarket
supervision nadzór
supplement opłata dodatkowa
suppository czopek
sure pewien
surfboard deska do serfowania
surname nazwisko
sweater sweter
sweatshirt bluza
sweet (taste) słodki
swelling opuchlizna
swim pływać
swimming pool basen
swimming trunks kąpielówki
swimsuit kostium kąpielowy
swollen spuchnięty

symptom (illness) objaw
synagogue synagoga

T

table stolik
take brać; **(carry)** zanieść; **(medicine)** brać; **(time)** trwać
take away [BE] na wynos
talk rozmawiać
tall wysoki
tampon tampon
tan opalenizna
tap [BE] kran
tapestry kilim
taxi taksówka
taxi rank [BE] postój taksówek
taxi stand postój taksówek
teacher nauczyciel
team drużyna
teaspoon łyżeczka do herbaty
teddy bear miś
telephone *n* telefon; *v* dzwonić
telephone bill rachunek telefoniczny
telephone booth budka telefoniczna
telephone call rozmowa telefoniczna
telephone number numer telefonu
tell powiedzieć

temperature temperatura
temple świątynia
temporarily tymczasowo
tennis tenis
tennis court kort tenisowy
tent namiot
tent peg kołek
tent pole maszt namiotowy
terminal terminal
terrace taras
terrible okropny
terrific wspaniały
tetanus tężec
text *n* **(phone)** sms; **(document)** tekst
thank *v* dziękować
thank you dziękuję
that to
theater teatr
theft kradzież
their(s) ich
theme park tematyczny park rozrywki
then (time) wtedy
there tam
thermometer termometr
these ci
they oni
thick gruby
thief złodziej
thigh udo

thin chudy
think myśleć
thirsty spragniony
this (one) ten
those tamci
thousand tysiąc
throat gardło
through przez
thumb kciuk
ticket bilet
ticket office kasa biletowa
tie krawat
tight *adv* ciasny
tights (clothing) rajstopy
time czas; **(exact time)** godzina
timetable [BE] rozkład jazdy
tin opener [BE] otwieracz do puszek
tire (car) opona
tired zmęczony
tissue chusteczka
to do
tobacco tytoń
tobacconist sklep tytoniowy
today dzisiaj
toe palec u nogi
toilet [BE] toaleta
toilet paper papier toaletowy
tomorrow jutro
tongue język
tonight dziś wieczorem
too (extreme) za

tooth ząb
toothache ból zęba
toothbrush szczoteczka do zębów
toothpaste pasta do zębów
top (head) góra
torn naderwany
tour wycieczka
tour guide przewodnik wycieczki
tour operator organizator
  wycieczki
tourist turysta
tourist office biuro informacji
  turystycznej
tow truck pomoc drogowa
towel ręcznik
tower wieża
town miasto
town center centrum
town hall ratusz
toy zabawka
track tor
traditional tradycyjny
traffic ruch
traffic jam korek
traffic light światła
traffic violation wykroczenie
  drogowe
trailer przyczepa
train pociąg
train station dworzec kolejowy
trained wykwalifikowany

tram tramwaj
transit (travel) przejazd
translate tłumaczyć
translation tłumaczenie
translator tłumacz
trash (garbage) śmieci
trash can śmietnik
travel *n* podróż; *v* podróżować
travel agency biuro podróży
travelers check czek podróżny
travelers cheque [BE] czek
  podróżny
tray taca
tree drzewo
trim *v* podstrzyc
trip wycieczka
trolley wózek
trousers spodnie
truck ciężarówka
true prawdziwy
try próbować
try on (clothes) przymierzyć
T-shirt t-shirt
tumor nowotwór
tunnel tunel
turn skręcić
turn down zmniejszyć
turn off wyłączyć
turn on włączyć
turn up (volume, heat)
  zwiększyć

TV telewizor
tweezers pinceta
twice dwa razy
twin bed łóżko podwójne
twist *v* **(hurt)** skręcić
type (sort) rodzaj
typical typowy
tyre [BE] opona

U

U.K. Wielka Brytania
U.S. Stany Zjednoczone
ugly brzydki
ulcer wrzód
umbrella parasol
uncle wuj
uncomfortable niewygodny
unconscious nieprzytomny
under pod
understand rozumieć
underwear bielizna
undress rozbierać (się)
uneven (ground) nierówny
unfortunately niestety
uniform mundur
unit (phone card) impuls
university uniwersytet
unleaded (gas) bezołowiowa
unlimited mileage bez limitu kilometrów
unlock otworzyć

unpleasant niemiły
unscrew odkręcić
urgent pilny

V

vacation wakacje
vacuum cleaner odkurzacz
vegetarian *adj* wegetariański; *n* wegetarianin
visa wiza

W

wait czekać
wallet portfel
water woda
week tydzień
where gdzie
white biały
window okno
window seat siedzenie przy oknie
wine list lista win
wireless bezprzewodowy
work *v* **(function)** działać; **(job)** pracować

X

X-ray rentgen

A

aktualny up-to-date
alarm przeciwpożarowy fire
  alarm
aleja boulevard
ambasada embassy
angielski English
Anglia England
antyki antiques store
aparat fotograficzny camera
apteka pharmacy
artykuły bezcłowe duty-free
  goods
aseptyczny antiseptic
astma asthma
atrakcja turystyczna tourist
  attraction
autokar long-distance bus [coach
  BE]
autostrada highway [motorway
  BE]

B

bagaż baggage
bagaż podręczny carry-on [hand
  luggage *BE*]
bagno marsh
balkon balcony (theater)
balsam po opalaniu after-sun
  lotion
bankomat ATM
basen dla dzieci children's pool
basen kryty indoor swimming pool
basen odkryty outdoor swimming
  pool
benzyna gas [petrol *BE*]
bez cukru sugar-free
bez tłuszczu fat-free
bezglutenowy gluten-free
bezołowiowy unleaded (gasoline)
bezprzewodowy wireless (internet)
bezzwrotny non-returnable
biblioteka library
biegać *v* run
biegówki cross-coutry skis
bielizna underwear
bilet ticket
bilet elektroniczny e-ticket
bilet grupowy group ticket
bilet okresowy season ticket
bilet parkingowy parking ticket
biuro office
biuro obsługi klienta customer
  service
biuro podróży travel agency
biuro rzeczy znalezionych lost-
  and-found [lost-property office *BE*]
biuro turystyczne tourist office

biznes business
biżuteria jewelry
błąd mistake
blokada lock (on a bike)
błyszczyk lipgloss
ból pain
budka autobusowa bus shelter
bungalow bungalow
but shoe
butelka bottle

C

cena price
centrum biznesu business district
centrum handlowe shopping mall
  [centre *BE*]
centrum miasta downtown area
  [town centre *BE*]
centrum odnowy biologicznej spa
centrum ogrodnicze garden center
chemiczna toaleta chemical toilet
chodnik sidewalk [pavement *BE*]
ciepły warm (water)
ciężarówka truck
ciężki heavy (luggage)
cło duty (customs)
cmentarz cemetery
cukiernia pastry shop
czasopismo magazine
czek check [cheque *BE*]
czek podróżny travelers check

[cheque *BE*]
czekać wait

D

dabingowany dubbed
dania dnia menu of the day
darowizna donation
data urodzenia date of birth
data ważności expiration [expiry
  BE] date
dawkowanie dosage
deklaracja celna customs
  declaration
delikatesy delicatessen
deska do windsurfingu
  windsurfing board
deska surfingowa surfboard
dieta diet
długopis pen
do until
do wynajęcia for rent [hire *BE*]
do żucia chewable (tablets)
dokładna reszta exact change
dom mieszkalny apartment building
dom towarowy department store
domowej roboty homemade
dostawa delivery
dostęp access
dowód tożsamości identification
dozorca caretaker
drewno wood

droga road

drzewo tree

drzwi automatyczne automatic doors

drzwi przeciwpożarowe fire door

dworzec autobusowy bus station

dworzec kolejowy train station

dzbanek pot (for tea)

działać v work

działanie uboczne side effect

dziecko child

dzień day

dzień powszedni weekday

dzisiaj today

E

e-mail e-mail

emeryt senior citizen

epilepsja epilepsy

epileptyk epileptic

F

fabryka factory

fajerwerk firework

faks fax

festyn fair

filharmonia concert hall

filiżanka cup

folia aluminiowa aluminum [kitchen *BE*] foil

formularz form

fotelik dziecięcy car seat

fryzjer hairdresser

funt pound (sterling)

G

gabinet dentystyczny dental office [surgery *BE*]

gabinet lekarski doctor's office [surgery *BE*]

galeria gallery

garnek pot (for cooking)

gaśnica fire extinguisher

gdzie where

giełda stock exchange

głęboko deep

godzina hour

godziny urzędowania business hours

godziny wizyt visiting hours

góra mountain

gorączka temperature

gość guest

gospodarstwo farm

gotować v boil

gotówka cash

H

hala targowa indoor market

hamulec bezpieczeństwa emergency brake

hasło password

I

ile how many,
how much
imię name
informacja information desk
informacja dla klientów
customer information
informacja o lotach flight
information
informacja o sklepie store
directory [guide *BE*]
instruktor instructor
internet internet
izba przyjęć emergency ward

J

jadalnia dining room
jakość quality
jaskinia cave
jasny light (color)
jeden one
jedwab silk
jedzenie na wynos to go [take-
away *BE*] (food)
jesień fall [autumn *BE*]
jeść eat
jezioro lake
jeździectwo horseback riding
język tongue (part of body);
language
język obcy foreign language

jubiler jeweler
jutro tomorrow

K

kafejka internetowa internet cafe
kamizelka ratunkowa life jacket
kantor currency exchange office
kapliczka shrine
kapsułka capsule (medication)
karetka ambulance
karta key card (hotel)
karta do telefonu phone card
karta kredytowa credit card
karta pokładowa boarding pass
(airport)
karta rabatowa discount card
karta win wine list
kasa biletowa ticket office
kasa ekspresowa express checkout
kasjer cashier
kask crash helmet
katedra cathedral
kaucja deposit
kawałek piece
klieliszek glass (alcoholic)
kierownik manager
kierunek direction (map)
kilometr kilometer
kiosk z gazetami newsstand
klasa biznes business class
klasa turystyczna economy class

klif cliff
klimatyzacja air conditioning
klimatyzator air conditioner
klinika clinic
kolejka linowa cable car
koło ratunkowe life preserver [belt BE]
komiks comic book
komisariat police station
kompresor air pump (gas station)
komputer computer
koncert concert
konkurs contest
kontaktować v contact
kontrola celna customs control
kontroler biletów ticket inspector
korek traffic jam
kościół church
kosmetyki cosmetics
koszerny kosher
kosztować v cost
koszyk shopping basket
kradzież theft
krajowy domestic (flight)
kran faucet [tap BE]
krem nawilżający moisturizer
krem z blokadą UV sunscreen
kropla drop (medication)
krwotok bleeding
książka telefoniczna directory
księgarnia bookstore

kucharz cook, chef
kuchenka mikrofalowa microwave
kuchnia kitchen
kurs wymiany exchange rate
kuszetka berth (train)
kwiaciarnia florist
kwiat flower
kwota amount (money)

L

lądować arrive (plane)
las forest
latarnia morska lighthouse
lato summer
lecieć v fly
lekarz doctor
lekki light (weight)
leżak deck chair
linia (lotnicza) airline
list polecony registered letter
list priorytetowy express mail
lista drinków drink menu
lokalny local
lot flight
loteria lottery
lotnisko airport
lotnisko krajowe domestic airport
lotnisko międzynarodowe international airport
lubić v like

Ł

łazienka bathroom
łopatka spatula
łódź ratunkowa life boat
łóżeczko dziecięce crib [child's cot *BE*]
łóżko bed
łyżka do odmierzania measuring spoon
łyżwiarstwo ice skating
łyżwy ice skates

M

mały small (size)
mapa drogowa road map
matka mother
mdłości nausea
mdły bland
meble furniture
mgła fog
miarka kuchenna measuring cup
miejsce seat (bus, train, plane)
miejsce na piknik picnic area
miejsce przy oknie window seat
miejsce przy przejściu aisle seat
miejsce urodzenia place of birth
miejsce zbiórki meeting place [point *BE*]
miejscówka reservation (train)
międzynarodowy international
mikrofalówka mircowave

miska bowl
mleczarnia dairy
młodzież youth
młyn windmill
mniej less
moczary swamp
mokry wet
mop mop
morze sea
motor motorcycle
motorower moped
mówić speak
msza mass
muzeum museum
mydło soap

N

na dole downstairs
na górze upstairs
na zewnątrz outside
nadbagaż excess baggage
namiot tent
napad mugging
napisać write
napiwek tip
naprawa *n* repair (car)
naprawić *v* fix (a car)
narty wodne water skis
następny next
nawierzchnia road surface
nawilżacz moisturizer

nazwisko last name
nazwisko panieńskie maiden
name
niedaleko close
niepalący non-smoking
nierówny uneven (surface)
noc night
nocleg accommodation
nocny dyżur night duty
nocny portier night porter
normalny normal
nowy new
numer kierunkowy country code
numer lotu flight number
numer miejsca seat number
numer pierwszej pomocy
emergency number

O

objazd detour [diversion *BE*]
obóz *n* camp
obozować *v* camp
od from (time)
odbiór bagażu baggage claim
oddział department
odebrać receive
odkurzacz vacuum cleaner
odlatywać leave
odprawa check-in (airport)
odprawa bagażu baggage check
odwołany cancelled

odzież damska ladieswear
odzież męska menswear
ognisko campfire
ograniczenie prędkości speed
limit
ogród garden
okazja bargain
okno window
okres period (of time);
menstruation
okulary glasses (optical)
okulary przeciwsłoneczne
sunglasses
opera opera
opis description
opłata bankowa bank charge
opłata obowiązkowa minimum
charge
opłata za dzień day charge
opłata za usługę service charge
opłata za wstęp admission charge
opóźniony delayed
optyk optician
ostry spicy
ostrzeżenie warning
otwarty open (shop)

P

paczka package [parcel *BE*]
paczka ekspresowa express mail
pakować pack

palacz smoker
paliwo fuel
pan sir
pani madam
panie ladies (toilet)
panna miss
panowie gentlemen (toilet)
papierowy ręcznik paper towel
paragon receipt
parasol umbrella [sunshade BE]
park narodowy national park
park publiczny public park
parking parking lot [car park BE]
parking podziemny underground
   garage
parking wielopoziomowy parking
   garage
parkometr parking meter
parkować v park
parter first floor [ground floor BE];
   orchestra [stalls BE] (theater)
pas lane
pasażer passenger
pasmo górskie mountain range
pawilon pavilion
pchać push
pchli targ flea market
peron platform
piasek sand
pić v drink
piekarnia bakery

pielęgniarka nurse
pieniądze money
pierwsza klasa first class
pierwsza pomoc emergency
   services; first aid
pierwsze piętro second floor [first
   floor BE]
pieszy pedestrian
piętro floor (level in building)
pigułka pill
pikantny spicy
pilny urgent
pismo periodical
piwnica basement
plac square
plasterek slice
plaża dla nudystów nudist
   beach
plecak backpack
plomba filling (dental)
płacić v pay
płeć sex (gender)
płyta kompaktowa CD
płytki adj shallow
pływać v swim
po południu p.m.
pociąg Intercity Intercity train
pociąg lokalny local train
początkujący beginner
poczekalnia waiting room
poczta post office

podarunek gift

podjazd ramp

podłoga floor

podobać się like

podpaska sanitary napkin [pad *BE*]

podróż powrotna round-trip [return trip *BE*] (ticket)

poduszka pillow

pokład deck (ship)

pokoje do wynajęcia rooms for rent [to let *BE*]

pokój room (hotel)

pole field

pole bitwy battle site

pole namiotowe camping

polecać recommend

policja police

policja drogowa traffic police

polisa ubezpieczeniowa insurance card [certificate *BE*]

Polska Poland

południe noon (time); south (direction)

pomiędzy between

pomnik monument

pomoc drogowa breakdown services

poranek morning

port port

portfel wallet

postój taksówek taxi stand [rank *BE*]

pościel sheets

potrzebny required

potwierdzenie confirmation

potwierdzić confirm

powiedzieć *v* say

powtórzyć repeat

poznać meet

pożar fire

północ midnight (time); north (direction)

półwysep peninsula

pracować *v* work

prać oddzielnie wash separately

prać ręcznie hand wash only

pralnia laundry

pralnia chemiczna dry-cleaner

prasować *v* iron

prawnik lawyer

prawo jazdy driver's license

priorytet express mail

progi rzeczne rapids

prognoza pogody weather forecast

prom ferry

proszę please

prowizja commission

prysznic shower

prywatny private

przebieralnia fitting room

przecena sale

przechowalnia bagażu baggage office

przeciek leak

przed before

przed południem a.m.

przedstawić introduce (someone)

przedział compartment

przejście path; aisle (plane)

przejście dla pieszych pedestrian crossing

przejście podziemne underpass

przejściówka adapter

przekaz pieniężny money order

przekąska appetizer [starter *BE*]

przepaść precipice

przepychacz plunger

przesiadać się change [transfer *BE*] (bus)

przesyłka package

przeszkadzać disturb

przetłumaczyć translate

przewodnik guide (person); guidebook

przyczepa trailer

przyloty arrivals (airport)

przymierzalnia fitting room

przystanek autobusowy bus stop

przystanek na żądanie on-demand stop

ptak bird

punkt widzenia view point

pusty vacant

R

rabat discount

ratownik lifeguard

ratusz town hall

recepta prescription

recycling recycling

ręcznie robione handmade

ręcznik towel

rejs cruise

reklama advertisment

rentgen X-ray

restauracja restaurant

reszta *n* change (money)

rezerwacja reservation

rezerwuar reservoir

robak bug

rogatka toll booth

rondel saucepan

rondo roundabout

room service room service

rower bicycle

rozkład jazdy schedule [timetable *BE*]

rozkładane łóżko cot

rozmowa na koszt rozmówcy collect call [reverse-charge call *BE*]

rozumieć understand

rura pipe (water)

rząd row (of seats, people)
rzeka river
rzeźnik butcher

S

sąd courthouse
sala hall (large public room)
sala konferencyjna conference room
sala zebrań convention hall
salon gier arcade
sam alone
samolot plane
sauna sauna
schowek na bagaż luggage locker
schronisko młodzieżowe youth hostel
ściana wall
ścieżka path
sekretarka secretary
serwetka napkin
sieć network (of computers); chain (of stores)
siedzenie seat
siedzenie przy korytarzu aisle seat
siedzenie przy oknie window seat
silnik engine
siłownia gym
skala scale
skała rock
skasować validate (ticket)

skipass ski pass
sklep store
sklep bezcłowy duty-free store
sklep mięsny butcher shop
sklep muzyczny music store
sklep osiedlowy convenience store
sklep papierniczy stationery store
sklep z narzędziami hardware store
sklep z zabawkami toy store
sklep ze zdrową żywnością health food store
skóra leather; skin
skręcić v turn
skrytka bagażowa luggage locker
skrzynka pocztowa mailbox [postbox BE]
skrzyżowanie intersection [junction BE]
skuter wodny jet-ski
ślepy zaułek dead end
śliski slippery
słony salty
śmieci trash [rubbish BE]
śniadanie breakfast
spa spa
śpiący policjant speed bump
spotkanie appointment (business); meeting (friends)
spóźniony late
stacja benzynowa gas [petrol BE] station

stacja kolejowa train [railway *BE*] station

stadion stadium

stal steel

stanowisko odprawy check-in desk (airport)

Stany Zjednoczone United States

startować take off, depart

statek ship

staw pond

steward flight attendant

stój codzienny casual clothing

stolik table

straż pożarna fire station

strażak firefighter

strój suit, clothing

strój wieczorowy evening dress

strój wizytowy formal dress

strumień stream

studiować *v* study

suszarka do włosów hairdryer

światła traffic light

światło light

święto państwowe national holiday

świeży fresh

szewc shoe repair [cobbler *BE*]

szklanka glass (non-alcoholic)

szkoła school

szlak trail

szpital hospital

T

tabletka tablet

taksówka taxi

talerz plate

targ market

telefon phone

telefon komórkowy cell phone [mobile phone *BE*]

telefon publiczny pay phone

telefonistka operator (phone)

terminal terminal

toaleta restroom [toilet *BE*]

tor track [platform *BE*]

tor wyścigowy racetrack [race course *BE*]

torebka purse [handbag *BE*]

trampolina diving board

trasa route

trasa autobusowa bus route

trawa grass

turystyka piesza hiking

tutaj here

tydzień week

tylko only

U

ubezpieczenie insurance

ugryzienie bite

ulepszony improved

ulica street

ulica jednokierunkowa one-way

street
uniwersytet university
unowocześniony modernized
usługa service
uwaga attention

W

w budowie under construction
w jedną stronę one-way (trip)
wagon car (train)
wagon restauracyjny dining car (train)
wakacyjny rozkład jazdy holiday schedule [timetable *BE*]
walizka suitcase
waluta obca foreign currency
warsztat samochodowy car mechanic [repair garage *BE*]
wąwóz gorge
wejście entrance; gate (at the airport)
wełna wool
wentylator fan (electric)
wesołe miasteczko amusement park
wewnętrzny extension (phone)
wiadomość news
widelec fork
więcej more
Wielka Brytania Great Britain
wieczór evening
wiedza knowledge
winda elevator [lift *BE*]

windsurfing windsurfing
wiosna spring
włączyć turn on
własność prywatna private property
woda water
wolno slowly
wolny free (place)
wolny pokój vacancy (accommodation)
wózek bagażowy luggage cart [trolley *BE*]
wpłata deposit
wschód east
wskazówka instruction
wspinaczka rock climbing
wstęp wolny admission free
wstęp wzbroniony no access
wybrzeże coast
wydarzenie event
wydrukować *v* print
wyjście exit; gate (at the airport)
wyjście bezpieczeństwa emergency exit
wyjście przeciwpożarowe fire exit
wyjście wzbronione no exit
wykręcić dial
wyłączyć turn off
wylogować się log off
wymiana exchange
wymiana walut currency exchange
wynajem samochodów car rental

[hire *BE*]
wypadek accident
wypłata cash withdrawal
wyprzedaż clearance
wyprzedzać *v* pass (car)
wysiąść get off (bus, train)
wysłać send
wysokie krzesełko highchair
występ show (in front of audience)
wzbroniony forbidden
wzgórze hill

Z

z napisami subtitled
zaawansowany advanced
zabawka toy
zachód west
zaczekać wait
zadzwonić call (phone)
zagraniczny international (flight);
    foreign (product)
zajazd guest house
zakaźny contagious, infectious
zakupy shopping
zalogować się log on
zamawiać *v* order
zamek castle (building); lock (door)
zamknięty closed (store)
zamówienie *n* order
zamrożony frozen
zamykać *v* lock

zapakować wrap
zapakować na prezent giftwrap
zaparcie constipation
zapinać fasten (seat belt)
zapłacony paid
zapominać forget
zarezerwować reserve (tickets)
zatkany blocked
zatłoczony crowded
zatoka bay
zatrzymać się stay (at a hotel);
    stop (not move)
zebra pedestrian crossing
zepsuty broken
zgwałcić *v* rape
zima winter
zimno *adv* cold
zimny *adj* cold
złoto gold
zły bad
znaczek stamp
znaczek pocztowy postage stamp
znaczyć mean (meaning)
znak drogowy road sign
zniżka discount
zwolnić slow down
zwrot pieniędzy refund
zwrotny returnable

Ż

żelazko *n* iron